The Films of Paul Morrissey

CAMBRIDGE FILM CLASSICS

General Editor: Raymond Carney, Boston University

Other books in the series:

The Films of
Paul Morrissey

MAURICE YACOWAR

CAMBRIDGE
UNIVERSITY PRESS

Published by the Press Syndicate of the University of Cambridge
The Pitt Building, Trumpington Street, Cambridge CB2 1RP
40 West 20th Street, New York, NY 10011–4211, USA
10 Stamford Road, Oakleigh, Melbourne 3166, Australia

First published 1993

Library of Congress Cataloging-in-Publication Data
Yacowar, Maurice.
The films of Paul Morrissey / Maurice Yacowar.
p.   cm. – (Cambridge film classics)
Includes bibliographical references and index.
Filmography: p.
ISBN 0-521-38087-1 (hc). – ISBN 0-521-38993-3 (pb)
1. Morrissey, Paul – Criticism and interpretation.   I. Title.
II. Series
PN1998.3.M685Y33   1993
791.43'0233'092 – dc20   92-40922
                                                        CIP

A catalog record for this book is available from the British Library

ISBN 0-521-38087-1 hardback
ISBN 0-521-38993-3 paperback

Transferred to digital printing 2004

All of the photographs and stills in this volume are published with the permission
of Paul Morrissey.

Contents

Acknowledgments

This book would not have been written without the support, encouragement, and resources of my home institution, Emily Carr College of Art and Design in Vancouver, B.C., Canada. I am especially grateful to my subject, Mr. Paul Morrissey, for his generosity in time, memories, resources, and help. I join the host of film writers indebted to Charles Silver and his dedicated staff at the Museum of Modern Art film archive. Finally, my thanks to my assistant, Cathy Johnson, for her help on this as on all my other work.

Introduction

Paul Morrissey may be America's most undervalued and least shown major director. In a career spanning more than twenty years he has made more than a dozen feature films of consistent weight and moral concern, with a distinctive aesthetic. While he has been often appreciated for individual films (or scenes), few writers have followed up on John Russell Taylor's 1975 assertion that the films Morrissey made for Andy Warhol "can stand comparison with anything else the cinema of today has to offer."[1] In the publishing splurge that followed Warhol's death and his Museum of Modern Art retrospective, Morrissey remained an obligatory name in passim but has hitherto not been accorded a full study.

Some reasons for this neglect are obvious. For one thing, Morrissey's doggedly personal course detached him from all film movements, major or minor. His views make him unique among American independent film-makers: he is a reactionary conservative. Aesthetically, his roots in Warhol's minimalism excluded him from both the commercial and the art-house mainstreams. Yet his faith in character, narrative, and the discriminating deployment of the cinematic apparatus also barred him from the avant-garde. Also, Morrissey stayed outside of the politics of the New York underground film movement. Though Robert Frank and Emile de Antonio were Warhol's friends and influences, neither Warhol nor Morrissey was involved in their New American Cinema Group, which convened in September 1960, or in any later derivative.[2] Morrissey proudly avers, "I'm totally independent of the independents."[3]

When Morrissey is mentioned in the Warhol retrospectives, it is often with resentment. Remnants of Warhol's entourage have not forgiven Morrissey for refusing to work with anyone using drugs or for otherwise introducing efficiency and order into the Factory, the large loft in which Warhol conducted his various art and social enterprises.[4] Gerard Malanga remembers Morrissey as Warhol's "sort of hatchet man." As superstar Viva remembers, Morrissey was "a real nine-to-fiver – the only one. He wanted to make money, be commercial. He dealt with the press. Paul could deal with everybody. He was quick...very quick. That's it. There was nobody else."[5] Stephen Koch recalls Morrissey as always "a kind of anomaly in the Factory," unlike all the refugees from the street culture: he was "a very typical young man in a hurry. That was not really the Factory style: Pushiness was out."[6]

Opinion is more dramatically divided on Morrissey's influence on Warhol's films. The Old Guard avant-garde contend that because of Morrissey, Warhol "quickly faded as a significant film-maker" after The Chelsea Girls (1966).[7] Or as Stephen Koch puts it, "something absolutely grotesque happened to Warhol's two finest gifts: his visual intelligence and his taste. It was simply this: Degradation."[8] (The gargantuan ten-day auction of Warhol's collection of some art and much junk in 1988 may undermine any such blanket assumption about Warhol's taste.)[9] Tony Rayns condemns Morrissey for "abandoning the formal integrity of Warhol's cinema and deliberately setting out to make films which would catch and hold an audience's interest." As if interesting an audience were not bad enough, Morrissey made "conventionally authored films...whose scripting and casting more or less explicitly express an authorial point of view – a mixture, as it happens, of prurience, condescension and supercilious contempt."[10]

To the astute John Russell Taylor, "the sign of Warhol's coming of age as a filmmaker has been his acceptance, around the time that his collaboration with Paul Morrissey began, of that basic axiom of the cinema, that what the camera really photographs is not the outside but the inside of people." Taylor continues: "The most immediate effect of Morrissey's influence might be regarded as 'going commercial.' Not that that seems to have been the prime intention; rather, Morrissey seems to be a much warmer, more outgoing person than Warhol, and his films therefore have a far more human touch."[11] In the same spirit, Madeleine Harmsworth in the Sunday Mirror heralded Morrissey's Flesh as "a film – unlike the others of Warhol's I have seen – of great humanity, even of innocence."[12]

As well as allegedly "selling out" to commercial film, Morrissey remained overshadowed by Warhol's celebrity. Although Morrissey was solely responsible for Flesh, Heat, and Trash, they still are often called Warhol films.[13] Films Warhol financed, but otherwise had nothing to do with, either creatively or consultorily, remain lumped into the Warhol canon. In an otherwise insightful study, David James misnames Morrissey's films Heat and Flesh for

Frankenstein as "remakes of specific films" and cites them as the third phase in *Warhol's* "analysis of the history of Hollywood."[4] The confusion over the films' authorship persists along with the uncertain authorship of much of Warhol's other work. For Warhol often farmed out his work to friends, family, and followers to finish or even to sign with his name.

More broadly, Peter Wollen suggests that Warhol assumed a machinelike impersonality in order to "enter, in phantasy, a world of pure seriality and standardisation." So "rather than producing images of commodities, he was repackaging packaging as a commodity in itself." Warhol reduced the identity of his subject "to the purely symbolic dimension of the name, functioning like a logo: 'Andy Warhol,' like 'Coca-Cola' or 'Walt Disney.'"[5] Though Warhol openly shrank from artist to logo, Koch calls Morrissey just Warhol's "collaborator" on even the "commercial sex farces" of which he acknowledges Morrissey is "their factual director, their creator, their energy."[6] Conversely, Morrissey sometimes serves as convenient scapegoat. Koch blames Morrissey for the new explicitness of Warholian pornography in *Blue Movie* (originally titled *Fuck*, 1968), of which Morrissey disapproved and with which (its star, Viva, confirms) he had nothing to do after setting up the lights and camera.[17]

It is probably inaccurate to speak even of "collaboration" in the Warhol–Morrissey films. In Parker Tyler's words, Warhol was at most "a filmic auteur by default," who "functioned with very little directorial power, leaving script and the coaching of actors largely to others, while using the paltriest methods of editing." Even on the scripted *Horse* (1965): "*Auteur! Auteur!* Where is the *auteur*? Only the stationary, faithfully grinding camera really remained in charge of affairs on this occasion at the Factory."[18] *My Hustler* (1965), commonly cited among Warhol's films as a turning point from the meditational toward the narrative, began with someone else's story but was enlivened by Morrissey's stylistic venturesomeness.[19]

Paul Morrissey was the presiding force of creative control in the "Warhol films" from *My Hustler* to *Lonesome Cowboys* (1967). The casting, cuing of actors, prompting of plot, arrangement of location, editing, and "whatever directing these films had, came from me," Morrissey avows. Morrissey even set the lights and prepared the camera; all Warhol had to do was operate it. With the advent of outside financing on *L'Amour* (1972), Warhol gave up even his minimal activity running the camera, turning it over to Jed Johnson, and withdrew from the set. The designers of the film's advertising gave the director's credit to Warhol. Warhol needed Morrissey's directing because "Andy was genuinely trying to explore though he couldn't say what. He was so flustered and so insecure about what was going to

3

happen that he was happy to leave all that to me." So, in fact, it was Morrissey and not Warhol of whom Antonioni approved: "His characters do and say what they want to and are, therefore, wholly original in contemporary films."[20] Morrissey says,

> There wasn't much direction in these experiments but whatever directing was done, I did. Andy just aimed the camera. It was Andy's notion – and it did grow into a kind of "concept" – that the camera should not be turned off. But I could see there was a law of diminishing returns, which Andy couldn't see. Once I was fully in the driver's seat, long before *Flesh*, then I went for more effects, with a story and longer shooting that I would then cut down. *Bike Boy, I, a Man,* all were done like that and then edited down.

Obviously Warhol had no influence on the films we will discuss here as Morrissey's. "Andy would just give me the money and let me do what I wanted. He had an encouraging tendency, always asking what he could do for you. Maybe *The Power of Positive Thinking* was the only book he ever read. He wasn't stupid but he didn't come across as intelligent. But he was. He knew what he could do and what he couldn't." According to Morrissey,

> Andy wasn't really capable of any kind of complicated thoughts or ideas. Ideas need a verb and a noun, a subject. Andy spoke in a kind of stumbling staccato. You had to finish sentences for him. So Andy operated through people who did things for him. He wished things into happening, things that he himself couldn't do. In that respect he was like Louis B. Mayer at MGM.

Morrissey suggests that

> Andy probably never even read the books written for him by others. Words were extremely difficult for him to put together or to deal with. He certainly never had any kind of aesthetic. Because he made so little sense, people were not only finishing sentences for him but inventing things that he might have meant and ascribing to him ideas he was unable to comprehend.

In David Ehrenstein's view, "Film, for Warhol, was a figure of social exchange, a network of private meanings made public, a field of free-flowing absolute research." Still, Ehrenstein reduces Morrissey's influence to the post-1967 "packaging" of Warhol's films.[21]

To his credit, Warhol did not claim the dubious film authorship he is given. When students at the University of California, Los Angeles, asked

4

Warhol exactly what he contributed to *Heat,* he replied, "Well, uh, I go to the parties."[22] Here is a typical Warhol interview, conducted by Joseph Gelmis:

GELMIS: How do you see your role in getting [an actor] to do what he does?
WARHOL: I don't do anything. That's what I don't understand.
GELMIS: What's your role, your function, in directing a Warhol film?
WARHOL: I don't know. I'm trying to figure it out.

Paradoxically, the more Warhol denied creating "his" films, the more he seems to have been credited with them – and with a becoming modesty! But Gelmis concludes that Warhol's "film primitivism may really be the natural expression of his vision of life."[23] In his eulogy, John Richardson called Warhol a "saintly simpleton."[24] Morrissey lays a strong claim to have directed the crowning achievements of "Warhol's cinema."

Morrissey's anonymity may also derive in part from one aesthetic principle he shared with Warhol, self-effacement – though Warhol managed to make his spectacular. Morrissey translated Warhol's antiemotional detachment into allowing the actor predominance over the film's director. As he described their early "experiments" to *The New York Times* in 1972, "Andy and I really try not to direct a film at all. We both feel the stars should be the center of the film. . . . When a movie is all one director's eye, it's devoid of life."[25] Morrissey rejected "cutting away from people and treating people like objects" for the more humanistic purpose, "to give the performers the films."[26] This was actually the crucial ethic in Morrissey's aesthetic. It resulted in what John Russell Taylor called "documentaries of the human spirit, of subjective rather than objective reality." Morrissey's works, Taylor says, "play scrupulously fair with their characters: the films do not build myths, they merely record them."[27] In attempting to revive the power of stars in Hollywood's heyday, Morrissey sometimes took an extreme position:

A couple of hundred years from now if you look back on the 20th century you will remember the movie stars. They are the people who truly dominate. Not Picasso with his dinky wall decorations which have no relation to people. People aren't genuinely interested in what he's done – and he's considered the greatest artist of the 20th century. People are interested in film and the performers. . . . I don't think they'll talk much about the directors. Or the painters. Or the writers. But I think Holly Woodlawn will be remembered.[28]

Be that as it may, Morrissey rejected the idea of "half-baked intellectuals ... that film is a vehicle for the director. Call it an old idea or an original idea – movies are vehicles for stars."[29] But not, Morrissey would add, for conventional actors. Morrissey based his cinema on the performances and improvisations of "nonactors" (but see the next section).

Out of respect, Morrissey allows his actors to define their characters' own terms for our compassion. Typically, in each film there is at least one scene in which a character's chatter suddenly turns back around us and we find ourselves feeling empathy for that person. It may be a whore's memory of a gang rape (in *Flesh*), a garbage lady's indomitable dignity (in *Trash*), an aging woman's pathetic need for her young stud (in *Heat*, so to speak), a vampire's craving for lost purity, or a tyrannical composer's brutish grasp for affection. Especially in the *Flesh* trilogy and in the costume (or "monster") movies, a monologue that begins in the remoteness of a squirming specimen ensnares our common humanity.

Morrissey's transvestite stars are especially effective in thus transcending their alienation. This is what prompted John Russell Taylor to call Morrissey/Warhol "sublimely unpatronizing." He continues: "They accept their 'stars' absolutely on their own terms; the stars are whatever they want to be, whatever they think they are, and that is that. They are not representative of anything but themselves. And after all, why should they be?" The transvestite actor Holly Woodlawn in *Trash* is an apt example: "As far as the film is concerned she is a woman, and so as far as we are concerned she becomes a woman too. In this performance the power of inner conviction overcomes any prosaic misgivings."[30] She remains persuasively a woman even when we see her quite male chest.

In two other senses Morrissey embraces human castoffs. In casting, he revived the forgotten thirties star Maurice Braddell (of *Things to Come*) for *Flesh* and *Women in Revolt*, and in *Spike of Bensonhurst* gave Ernest Borgnine one of his last good roles. Geraldine Smith, Joe's wife in *Flesh*, resurfaces as the whore Toni in *Mixed Blood* and again as the hero's mother in *Spike of Bensonhurst*. Morrissey doesn't have a company of performers but he remembers the forgotten. More important, he respects humanity that others spurn.

Kathy Acker finds Morrissey politically effective, as well. Acker believes that his films "made the art world, then the United States generally, accept, even admire those whom they had formerly condemned: drag queens, strippers, young homeless kids, not hippy pot smokers but actual heroin addicts and welfare victims."[31] In this respect Warhol seemed also to speak for Morrissey when he described members of his entourage as "leftovers of show business" who are "inherently funny": "I usually accept people on the basis of their self-images, because their self-images have more to do with the way they think than their objective-images do."[32] To reveal and to cast them, then, was to accept them, in a way as humanist as it was filmic. As Morrissey told Neal Weaver, "With us, people can be whatever they are, and we record it on film. If a scene is just a scene, with a lot of ideas that have nothing to do with the people, you don't need to make a movie, you could just type it."[33]

Morrissey's valued performers were generally of two opposite styles. Some were histrionic, relishing the chance to "act" as flamboyantly on-camera as off, most notably as the transvestites Holly Woodlawn and Candy Darling. Morrissey's transvestites, like the other Warhol "superstars," were already well-known New York presences who were invited to drop in to "perform" in front of the camera. At the other extreme, his early features rotated around the handsome but unexpressive Joe Dallesandro, a passive object of predatory and voyeuristic attention.

The eighteen-year-old Dallesandro happened by John Wilcock's apartment, which Warhol and Morrissey had borrowed to shoot *Loves of Ondine* (a ninety-minute excerpt from the twenty-four-hour * * * *). To enliven the flagging film, between reel changes Morrissey invited Dallesandro to portray Ondine's physical education instructor. His interplay with Ondine and Bridget Polk so improved the film that Morrissey used Dallesandro again in *Lonesome Cowboys*. Dallesandro was widely approved as a new spirit in the Warhol films. David Bourdon found him unique "because he lacked even the slightest trace of self-mockery or campiness."[34] As the more orthodox director George Cukor pointed out, "Joe Dallesandro does some enormously difficult things – walking around in the nude in a completely unselfconscious way.... [In *Trash*] He really made me understand, more than any other film, what a drug addict was."[35]

Morrissey continues to cast both the histrionic and the inarticulate. As late as *Beethoven's Nephew* (1985), he starred a veteran of the Molière theater (Wolfgang Reichmann) as Beethoven, and a handsome medical student (Dietmar Prinz) as the nephew. In *Spike of Bensonhurst* (1988) Morrissey cast the scene-chewing veteran Ernest Borgnine against the natural Sasha Mitchell. From both extremes Morrissey draws performances generous in either nuance or flash.

But "performances" they most definitely are. "None of my central characters – neither Joe nor the kids in *Forty-Deuce* or *Mixed Blood* or Spike or the Nephew – ever behaved in front of the cameras as they did in real life. They were usually happy and talkative but I'd tell them not to smile.

I wouldn't tell them what to do or think, I'd leave that to them. But I always say, 'No, one more time, but don't smile.' A smile is a kind of surrender to fate. It eliminates any kind of tension. It implies acceptance and therefore a kind of commitment." During the shooting of *Trash,* Morrissey instructed Dallesandro: "Stop the Method moping – just talk. And whatever you do, don't smile unless you *don't mean it!*"[36]

Morrissey rejects the entire tradition of Method acting as an aberration: "A John Wayne – who I think is the greatest screen artist – doesn't change his personality for the part" any more than a Rembrandt would feel an obligation to paint as Van Dyke or as Hogarth. The Method actor, like Paul Muni, "is an actor, not an artist, a sort of journeyman craftsman – and very uninteresting." Morrissey preferred to cast "people whose reactions on film are as close to their own personalities as they would be in real life." Morrissey told his American Film Institute audience that "anybody can take film. Anybody can edit film. The hard thing is to appear in front of the camera and be interesting. I think you're either interesting or you're not. I don't think anybody can learn to be interesting in front of a camera. That's the part of filmmaking that is a mystery."[37]

Morrissey bristles at interviewers who call his performers nonactors. "We don't handle non-actors," he says. "Everybody we handle is an actor. . . . We're proud of our films because they have such great performances in them. . . . acting in the great 'star' notion of acting – people living close to the reality of their personality."[38] Perhaps not surprisingly, Morrissey admires Ronald Reagan: "Reagan never had to invent himself. He's the same now as he was in movies in 1937."[39] At the beginning, "William Holden was awkward and mannered but Reagan was never self-conscious. He projected what he had perfectly."[40] "He's the kind of actor I like and the kind of politician I like. There's a connection."

Morrissey's actors were so convincing that their "performances" were often overlooked. But, he says, "The films were experiments in character. Neither of us wanted the people to be themselves in front of the camera. We weren't trying to make goddam documentaries." He resents Shirley Clarke's *Portrait of Jason* (1967) because "it exploited this guy. She got him drunk in front of the camera so he'd cry for her. And she thought she was following us! Didn't she realize our people were acting? They were improvising. It was all artificial, all performance." Paradoxically, the only scene in which the artifice of performance is explicitly referred to – Ondine flipping out while playing Pope in *The Chelsea Girls* (1966) – has fed the myth that the Warhol films simply recorded the actors' lives. So did the fact that Morrissey's characters tended to have their performer's names. But that convention began with John Cassavetes's ground-breaking *Shadows* (1959). As David James explains, "The close identification between actor and role, in which the actors' use of their own names implies that the situations they rehearse are personally felt rather than professionally assumed, is supposed to empower their fictional interaction with the added energy and credibility of the quasi-therapeutic working through of real-life relationships."[41] The new cinema's realism and its adaptation of cinema verité technology conspired to make Morrissey's composed, albeit exploratory, fictions seem to be accidents of reality.

The rich ambiguities around Morrissey's transvestites have particularly drawn insightful comment – though it's usually attributed to Warhol instead. For Gregory Battcock, this "sexual dualism as represented on the screen can be taken as further proof of Warhol's [*sic*] intent to unmask the sexual fraud of the contemporary cinema. The usual presentation of sex is a product of the art of packaging technology and it is illusion, facade, and gesture that we buy."[42] For Stephen Koch, the bisexual hustler and the transvestite in Warhol's (or Morrissey's) work are "linked for all their apparent difference by a common obsession with the mystery of how a man inhabits his flesh." Where the transvestite "builds a life upon the denial of his anatomical reality" the hustler "proclaims himself to be 'just a body.' " The former, as if a pure psyche, transcends his flesh; the latter reduces himself to flesh, but both embody the same dilemma.[43] For David James, where the male hustlers seem to absent themselves from their bodies when they assume the female function of passive visual/sexual object, "the transvestites need to maximize rather than minimize their presence. Their acting consequently is a hyperbolic, highly gestural pastiche of fragments of different codes of femininity, with the interaction between the different degrees of it and the various vocabularies for it being the source of multiple narrative ironies."[44]

Morrissey's nonscripted cinema thrived on the transvestite performers, who of necessity had been living out a role (in their case, the wrong gender) and so did not need a script to feed them lines or a self. Moreover, their exuberant exhibitionism was perfect for Morrissey's noninterventionist aesthetic. It also provided an intense psychological arena for Morrissey's cinema to explore. Finally, their sharp wit and minds often produced astonishing twists and revelations. Morrissey fed his actors lines between takes, then let them extemporize around their specific subjects, or more precisely, pour out their style until a soul gleamed forth. "My films are different in being largely 'uncinematic,' " Morrissey says. "I like nonstop dialogue. I seldom show anybody just doing something. I want people always talking."

Rather than script his films, Morrissey would film the actors' improvised chatter, then edit the scene down to the core that he would discover in his actors' creation. As Viva recalls, "The script in the Warhol–Morrissey movies was the common body of experience vibrating in the space between the actors. The success of the films was dependent on our ability to summon our lives' experiences to the front of our brains, the tips of our tongues, so tangible as to be almost visible out in front of our craniums."[45] Morrissey's strategy of filming his performers' improvisation differed from the other great American independent, John Cassavetes, for whom improvisation was a mode of rehearsal before filming began. As Morrissey gained confidence, experience, and a budget, he began to plan and even script his films. But even his most polished works – *Mixed Blood, Beethoven's Nephew,* and *Spike of Bensonhurst* – retain the flavor of the freshly spoken. Free from any obvious script or directorial fist, Morrissey's cinema refines what Louis Marcorelles called "lived" language.[46]

Even with his nontransvestite performers, when Morrissey began one of these early films he did not know where his performers' invention would lead him:

> I don't have any preconceived ideas of who the characters are. I just give the actors general, cliché parts to play and I find they put in lots of nuances that a writer wouldn't come up with. That's why I always like new actors or fresh ones, young ones, people who haven't done too much, because they have more new things to offer in the way of characterization. There's nobody who makes films, I think, in quite such an irresponsible way.[47]

Furthermore, as David James remarks,

> Both the personae assumed in the fictional narratives and the more consistent if not more real personae the actor assumed in everyday life remained unstable. Consequently, the drama of the Warhol narratives, even through the most 'commercial' of the Morrissey collaborations, resides in the interplay between the different levels of artifice in any one actor/character as much as in the interaction between the characters, even though each is a means of production of the other. Up to *The Chelsea Girls* and * * * *, the primary interest lay in people assuming roles; subsequently, as genre and narrative provided more stable fictional frames, it lay in people falling out of them.[48]

In a tradition that began with Robert Frank and Alfred Leslie's *Pull My Daisy* (1960), Warhol (that is, Morrissey) relentlessly anatomized "the inauthenticity of self-representation by recognizing that improvisation is a condition of being, and that identity is only an artifice."[49]

Revolting against artistic pretensions, Morrissey deliberately set out to make *"unimportant* films," with "the director as unimportant as possible."[50] He was equally unassuming in eschewing the art cinema audience: "Degenerates are not such a great audience, but they're a step up from the art crowd; we would always rather play a sexploitation theatre than an art theatre."[51] Morrissey rejected the freedom and fashions of sixties art, the epic egotism of the abstract expressionists, the happenings, fluxus, pop art, minimalism, the psychedelicatessen of the pop cults, indeed anything that seemed to abandon the moral rigor and formal accessibility of traditional art. He once told a German interviewer, "There's an English word for people who think [Warhol's] *Empire* is the height: It is 'snob.' "[52] This is the flip side of Morrissey's supposed "degradation" of Warhol's cinema. It might be called integrity.

Both Morrissey's ethics and aesthetics prevented him from asserting a strong directorial persona. Long after *"Andy Warhol Presents Flesh,"* Morrissey's first independent commercial ventures were initially advertised as *Andy Warhol Presents Dracula* and *Andy Warhol Presents Frankenstein.* (The later ads were shortened to *Andy Warhol's Dracula,* etc.) Warhol allowed his friend's films his famous imprimatur in order to ease their way into the marketplace, but this generosity helped to delay the recognition of Morrissey's own voice and values.

And voice and values are what distinguish the Morrissey canon. They are not the voice and values one expects from someone associated with the Warhol Factory, whether its hippie license or its minimalist aesthetic. For Morrissey is an artist of uncompromising moral values. As he puts it, his main theme has always been "people trying to survive all the freedoms they have been cursed with." He has stuck by his rigorous creed for all this time, unlike more compromising filmmakers.[53] Morrissey may be the last (if not indeed the only) of the red-hot puritans in the American independent cinema.

This paradox of the Puritan in the Flesh Factory may tempt one to charge Morrissey with sensationalism and duplicity. One might look for a conflict between Morrissey's didactic reflections and the charged imagery of his films. His work may suggest a vicarious fascination with nudity, gutter language, the squalor of the drug subculture and the sordid uses of the flesh. But does Morrissey serve the devil he condemns? Rather than a moralistic innovator in the underground, is Paul Morrissey the poor man's Cecil B. DeMille, who wallows in the orgies around the golden calves, then covers himself with a pat pontification?

The answer is no. The gap between the fabric of Morrissey's films and his stated morality disappears when his films are openly experienced. Morrissey's humanist morality is clear in his respect for his performers and his submission to their intuitions and revelations. Morrissey by reflex embraces the sinner even as he condemns the sin. His obsession is not with the spectacle of squalor but with the pathos of a wasted humanity. If he returns and returns to intense images of the sordid life, it is in the spirit of the Juvenalian satirist, who feels so passionately the horror of his vision that he rages against the folly he surveys. Morrissey is no more hypocritical in his moral focus than Swift was, another intensely moral man given to scabrous representations of the corruptions of his time. This reiterated rigor and consistent morality distinguish Morrissey from Warhol's aesthetic nihilism.

Morrissey has remained as committed to traditional narrative as to morality. As he recalls, during his early film years, "If it didn't make any sense it was art, but I was always a narrative film-maker." Because "My films were silent, with a narrative, not avant-garde Jonas Mekas-type movies.... no-one heard of me."[54] Where the underground's new poetic cinema exulted in abstraction and fantasies, Morrissey clung to his commitment to character. So out of Warhol's Factory came – paradoxically – a traditional narrative filmmaker who advanced the rhetoric and audience of experimental film but who railed against permissiveness and the abandonment of traditional values.

Morrissey's traditionalism gleams through all his studies of life in the American underbelly, whether the Los Angeles narcissists or the drug-numbed New York street kids. It is also reflected in his Madison Avenue apartment, with his careful collection of mission furniture and Rookwood pottery, acquired twenty years ago, long before it became fashionable. He also has a large collection of photogravure travel books from the nineteenth century and the 1920s, with richly detailed images recorded by 8 × 10 cameras.[55] Everything he collects draws him with its special, almost obsolete, character, but also by the fact that it has not yet been espoused by other collectors. He preserves what others overlook. Whether in his library, his decoration, his aesthetics, or in the characterization and values in his films, Paul Morrissey recoils from the throwaway culture and reaffirms the value of the discarded.

I

The Life and Work

Paul Morrissey was born on February 23, 1938, in Manhattan. His father was a Bronx lawyer. An ancestor founded the Drummond detective agency, which was a forerunner of the Secret Service in Lincoln's day, and which provided the model for the fictional Bulldog Drummond. On his mother's side, the Morans, an uncle was vice-mayor under John F. Hylan in the twenties and became the mayor's scapegoat in a scandal involving pavement blocks. Paul has one sister and three brothers, the latter all independents in small construction businesses. "Like me, they don't like working for others."

He grew up in Yonkers, across from the Woodlawn section of the Bronx. His turf was a unique enclave, separated from the city by natural boundaries on all sides: the Bronx River Valley, Van Cortlandt Park, and the huge Woodlawn cemetery. The moral and psychological function of the urban landscape became important themes in his *Flesh* trilogy and in his later street life features, *Forty-Deuce, Mixed Blood,* and *Spike of Bensonhurst.*

Morrissey was educated entirely within the Catholic system, which he considers "the best thing that ever happened to me." Nuns taught him for eight years – well and toughly – at St. Barnabas School. He continued under almost totally Jesuit tutelage at Fordham Prep and at Fordham University, where he majored in English. Morrissey dismisses as "a grotesque absurdity" the representation of the Catholic school system as sadistic rote learning. On the contrary, he found that the dedicated teachers could bring the best out of any student. Further, "Without institutionalized religion as the basis, a society can't exist. In my lifetime, I've seen this terrible eradication of what makes sense and its replacement by absolute horror. All the sensible values of a solid education and a moral foundation have been flushed down the liberal toilet in order to sell sex, drugs, and rock and roll."

Though Morrissey's moral vision remains rooted in his Catholic upbringing, he considers himself less of a Catholic today than Warhol was.[1]

> Andy always went to church. I can't stand it any more. It's appalling to see the hippie service they give with all that English and holding hands and the chalice of wine. All this hippie garbage in what used to be a wonderful religion. I'm not a "religious Catholic." I just think it's good common sense. By some accident I was part of it. It didn't seem wonderful at the time. It was just sensible. Now I see it was wonderful. I still believe every word of what they told me then. Nothing of what they tell me now. "Liberal" is to me the most hateful word in the English language.

Indeed he appreciates the Soviets for suppressing liberalism, rock and roll, and other modish fatuousness. In 1993 he can draw scant comfort from seeing Western libertinism sweep across Eastern Europe under the flag of MacFreedom.

While at college, Morrissey frequented the screenings at MOMA. He was especially influenced by the German cinema of the twenties and thirties, when the medium was stretched to serve the passionate social concerns of the expressionists. In contrast, Morrissey finds Fassbinder's genius to have lain mainly in raising public funds from the German bureaucracy for self-indulgent, nonthreatening melodramas. Morrissey's favorite German film since the fifties is Ulrich Edel's uncompromising *Christiane F.:* "It showed real people with real problems. It wasn't comforting like Fassbinder's homage to popular genres or the fantasies of Wenders and Herzog."

Among English-language directors, Morrissey singles out Carol Reed ("ten times the director Hitchcock was"). Reed is a kindred spirit for his commitment to narrative and characterization but primarily for his fascination with the innocent face of evil. From Reed, Morrissey learned "that you could tell exactly the same story over and over with the same kind of uncommitted central character, being both realistic and metaphorical at the same time. I saw all his films thirty or forty times on TV and I still watch them." From Reed's extraordinarily intense commitment to his films, Morrissey learned "how films should be made," free from the commercial cinema's demands to work with producers or stars.

> I also borrowed from him the central hero who's not a hero, but one who is compromised by the period he lives in, postwar Europe or urban squalor, a setting of violence and/or death, and the use of foreign-accented actors to both increase characterization and to sug-

Morrissey among the liberals. Morrissey can be spotted in the left background, having attached himself to John Kennedy's entourage for a day. The supporting cast includes Herbert Lehman, John F. Kennedy, Adlai Stevenson, and (right background) Bess Myerson.

gest an alienated hero (for example, in *Frankenstein, Dracula, Madame Wang's,* and *Mixed Blood*).

Morrissey "recycled" one compelling image from Reed's *The Third Man* (1949): The naive hero (Joseph Cotten) and the corrupt one (Orson Welles) finally confront each other – in a sewer! "This notion that the conflicts of modern life, so debased and degenerate, are fittingly placed in the ultimate setting of human waste, was an idea that never left me," Morrissey says. "The idea that modern life is predicated upon toilet values and is appropriately presented in actual toilets recurs in almost every film I've ever made."

Morrissey stumbled into the film art-cum-industry when his hunt for an apartment led him into the East Village. He rented a vacant store, where he slept and ate – and started to run 16 mm films on a rented projector for audiences perched on rented chairs. "Like many Hollywood studio heads,

The exhibitor: Paul Morrissey at his cinema at 36 East 4th Street, c. 1961–62.

I began in the Lower East Side as an operator of a Nickelodeon," albeit fifty years later. He bought a Bolex and started to shoot the odd film for his programs. The police closed down his operation after a few months for his lack of a license.

Some sense of Morrissey's now-unavailable films can be inferred from their brief description in the third *Film-Makers' Cooperative Catalogue.*[2] *Ancient History* is a rearrangement of a ten-year-old newsreel. *Dream and Day Dream* is succinctly called "A fooling around in front of the camera type of film." *Mary Martin Does It* parodies a clean-up commercial that featured Mary Martin. In Morrissey's version, a pretty girl goes about putting garbage in garbage cans. But she also poisons the neighborhood bums with booze, after entrapping them with outdoor living-room sets of trash furniture. An older bag lady, who empties the garbage cans, sees the girl's murders, chases her, then throws her under a large street sweeper. Clearly the film owes more to the Morrissey of *Trash* than to the Mary Martin canon. In a 1963 short, *Taylor Mead Dances,* the brilliant member of the Warhol entourage takes his white Rolls Royce to Second City, where he does a dance with tin cans. Stanley Fisher commissioned *Peaches and Cream,* a documentary about his collage paintings, and *Merely Children,* a

16

home movie of Fisher's children at play. In *Like Sleep* two young drug addicts turn on and drift into sleeplike stupor – a familiar Morrissey theme. In *About Face,* Karen Holzer "walks, then turns around and walks in the opposite direction." In *The Origin of Captain America,* Morrissey intercuts comic book pages with Joseph Diaz reading them. These films run between five and forty-five minutes long. His one early feature, *Sleep Walk,* seventy minutes, is described as "a somewhat slow and lengthy film, in which someone walks about, meets and talks with other people, and ends up dead... in which nothing is heard, but only seen, the dialogue having been omitted."

The catalog describes *Civilization and Its Discontents* as featuring "much serious walking about." In fact, several blackly comic anecdotes are counterpointed to lyrical visuals: a hood in a pea jacket strangles a fat albino in Cooper Square; a flower-bearing young man climbs out of a garbage scow and watches a girl jump into the Hudson River. The whimsical scenes gain seriousness from the Freud title. According to Donald Lyons, this short anticipates *Spike of Bensonhurst:* Both are "about a cleansing energy applied to a fallen world. But this time the mode is self-mocking satire. A poet of lye and laughing gas, Morrissey has concocted a new genre: slapstick neorealism."[3]

After tentative jobs in insurance and working in Spanish Harlem for the New York Welfare Department (presaging the social worker's visit in *Trash*), Morrissey became involved with Warhol. Earlier, when he dropped in on the first public screening of Warhol's *Sleep,* he found it "cute. Interesting. But I only stayed for about an hour." When he later visited the filming of *Space* (1965), an Edie Sedgewick scene never released, his advice led to Warhol's first use of a camera movement. In Tony Rayns's view, with his first pan, Warhol forever lost the authenticity of mechanical autonomy in his film work because it was "the first directorial intervention in the process of Factory film-making."[4] As Morrissey stayed around, he exerted increasing influence and assumed more responsibilities, not just on the Warhol films but by bringing a new efficiency to the operation of the Factory. As he recalls, Morrissey was so important that Warhol gave him a management contract for a 25 percent commission of everything Warhol received. The contract was signed at the time Morrissey undertook a major project, discovering and managing the rock group The Velvet Underground, under Warhol's nominal sponsorship.

In 1965, Broadway producer Michael Myerberg offered to pay Warhol to bring his glamour and entourage to a new disco that was about to open in a converted plane hangar in Queens. To justify Warhol's attendance, Morrissey suggested they find a rock group that Warhol would sponsor and that would play at the disco's opening. He also proposed running some of the film footage they had been shooting at the Factory, in order to generate some money from these noncommercial experiments. Managing a rock group would also improve Warhol's cash flow, Morrissey suggested. Myerberg and Warhol agreed, so Morrissey had to find Andy a group.

He found one. Morrissey accompanied Gerard Malanga to a photo shoot for The Velvet Underground. Morrissey was immediately struck by the group's androgynous drummer, Maureen Tucker, and by the eccentricity of John Cale's electric viola. The first group Morrissey visited, he chose immediately, trusting (as always) his instinct – and luck – in casting. Morrissey also proposed adding Nico (a beautiful singer Fellini had introduced in *La Dolce Vita*) as a lead singer: "The group needed something beautiful to counteract the kind of screeching ugliness they were trying to sell, and the combination of a really beautiful girl standing in front of all this decadence was what was needed."[5] To prepare for the disco opening, from February 8–13, at the Film-Makers' Cinémathèque on West 41st Street, The Velvet Underground performed a multimedia rock show with Nico, dancing by Malanga and Edie Sedgewick, and films by Warhol and Morrissey, all advertised under the title *Andy Warhol, Up-tight*. Myerberg dropped his original plan to promote his disco and opened with The Rascals instead. But Morrissey arranged for the group's presentation at the Dom on St. Mark's Place, where they opened under the name Exploding Plastic Inevitable, adjectives skimmed off of "amphetamine Bob Dylan gibberish liner-notes" to the album *Bringing It All Back Home*.[6]

Morrissey also produced the group's first album, for a couple of thousand dollars and three or four nights of studio time; the disk remains available twenty-five years later. Morrissey shepherded the group for its show at The Trip in Los Angeles and on an arduous bus tour. A photograph of the landmark L.A. performance appears in Marshall McLuhan's *The Medium is the Massage*, with this text: "History as she is harped. Rite words in rote order."[7] McLuhan cites their light show as a recovery of primordial emotions through acoustic space. When the Underground decided to suspend their performances until their album made them stars, Morrissey arranged first for Tim Buckley, then for the young Jackson Browne, making his debut, to play guitar for Nico's solo show. Shortly after, the group left Warhol to escape the art circuit. Morrissey also launched Warhol's *Inter/View* magazine and co-edited *Andy Warhol's Index Book* (Random House, 1967), a "throwaway" that now sells for more than a thousand dollars. Still, Morrissey's importance in the Warhol canon has never been fully acknowledged, save by those who blame him for Warhol's commercial sellout. Morrissey was, then, largely responsible for the three things for which Warhol became most known to the general public: the rock group, the magazine – and especially the films.

Morrissey emphasizes that the early short films he made for Warhol were not films but "experiments." The titles were catchphrases made up afterward so that the film cans could be labeled on the shelf.

The idea these scenes were movies is wrong. It attributes to Andy a sense of purpose that's not quite accurate. We used a double screen for *More Milk Yvette* because the reels were too weak on their own. When they came back from the lab we screened them. Sometimes I loaded two projectors at the same time and if one was too boring I turned on the other at the same time, to get it over with. But once we stumbled upon this, we could see they worked better simultaneously. These were all simple ideas. They were not conceived as some grand artistic design.

The "films" were just

experimental scenes, generated by Andy's curiosity about what would happen and his desire to avoid taxes and to get his name out to the public beyond the art gallery world. There was no money in the art gallery world then. To make a name for yourself as an artist you had to get your name in the paper. Even now, in modern art people only buy the name, not the actual art. "That's a Picasso," but a Picasso what? Andy wanted to get away from Leo Castelli, who was giving him a thousand dollars a week in exchange for fifty percent of whatever Andy's pictures sold for. Andy wanted to go to another dealer who would just take ten.

To Morrissey, the experiments

were what Edison would have made if he had invented sound film instead of silent. They were just one-reel improvisations of the actors. I knew they were primitive, regressive. I looked on them as parallels of the first novels, those epistolary novels by Richardson and Smollett. These separate letters would fall together and you'd have a novel coming together. A letter is something inconsequential or trivial but when they are all put together, they become something more. That's what our little films of separate scenes would do. After all, I didn't sleep through *all* my English classes at college.

19

Always with Morrissey, the formal or aesthetic issue segues into a moral one.

> Andy was right with his theory of limits. In order to make art you need limits. But Andy was just not capable of imagining something and then getting it, or even arranging for someone to get it for him. So in these basically undirected movies, whatever direction it had – in story, in casting, in dialogue subject – it was due to me. The nice thing was, Andy would never say no. He'd always say "great" because he was so relieved I had an idea for him. I had total autonomy. I was embarrassed how much autonomy I had. Andy aimed the camera but his participation virtually ended when we got to wherever we were shooting.

As Morrissey recalls, it was he who thought of pulling together twelve one-reel scenes of people talking in rooms that looked like hotel rooms and running them as one film, when Jonas Mekas needed a program for his Cinémathèque. That became the epochal *The Chelsea Girls*, "Warhol's" double-screen breakthrough film. As Merle Oberon had just played a duchess in *Hotel* and Bridget Polk was always called "The Duchess," the hotel idea pulled the scenes together. Warhol preferred *The Chelsea Girls* as a title instead of *Hotel Chelsea* so that the structure would not seem too logical: "Andy thought that if it had any logic then it wasn't art. He resented people saying it was about people in a hotel. That made too much sense for him." But

> *Chelsea Girls* was never a movie. It was different scenes I set up as promising. They were intended to give Andy something to film in the nonstop thirty-minute format, so he could spend two or three hundred dollars a week on filming so he wouldn't have to pay taxes on it. The scenes were a combination of my giving them some direction when the camera was stopped and the actors' improvisation. Once the camera started rolling, for thirty-five minutes (the length of the reel) they really directed themselves.

The Chelsea Girls brought a new respectability to the underground cinema. It won a national recognition far beyond the places it actually played. Jonas Mekas trumpeted it as "an epic movie-novel" which "in its complex and overlapping structures, in its simultaneity of lives before our eyes, comes closest to Joyce." With the classical grandeur of Victor Hugo, Mekas said, "It is a tragic film. The lives that we see in this film are full of desperation, hardness, and terror," and the actors "are totally real, with their transformed, intensified selves."[8] Andrew Sarris was more reserved: "Nevertheless a meaningful form and sensibility emerges through all the apparent arrogance and obfuscation.... Warhol's people are more real than real because the camera encourages their exhibitionism. They are all 'performing' because their lives are one long performance and their party is never over."[9] Made for less than $3,000, the film grossed about $130,000 in its first five months in New York, then wended its way to theaters in Los Angeles, Dallas, Washington, San Diego, and Kansas City. It was banned in Boston, then invited to the Cannes festival but at the last minute banned.[10]

The Chelsea Girls was the first full flowering of the Warhol personality film – and it was coaxed out and tempered and pulled together – that is to say, directed – by Morrissey. Indeed, during his breakdown, Ondine specifically addresses Morrissey because that's who was directing: "I'm ready to get any kind of confession, Paul. Anyone who wants to confess may confess."[11] (He wanted Morrissey to send in another actor.)

As Morrissey recalls,

Andy was an entrepreneur who wanted to produce something. I was the experimenter who created the experiments for him and then learned from the films that were made. I learned that really interesting personalities were out there and the trick is to let those personalities come out in front of the camera. I'm not consciously thoughtful when I make a film. I'm most concerned with what personality will come out in the film. I developed a sense of what works with people in front of the camera and what won't. The best proof something is happening is when the audience laughs." The Morrissey film has been comic ever since.

Morrissey also directed *Lonesome Cowboys,* but says,

I feel it's too silly. It was a real exception, the first film I thought would be a production of sorts. We shot it in sixteen millimeter with a big budget, for us, between four and five thousand dollars. We all went out on location to Old Tucson. I rented this cowboy village, that John Wayne was one of the owners of. I had this idea of doing *Romeo and Juliet* with groups of cowboys and cowgirls. But no girls came because they had a quarrel with Viva. We made the film over a Friday morning, Saturday and Sunday morning.

This rather outrageous parody has its charms. A cowboy (Eric Emerson) does his ballet exercises at the ol' hitchin' post, the better to hold up his holster; he avows, "It builds up the buns." Other cowpokes cattily discuss

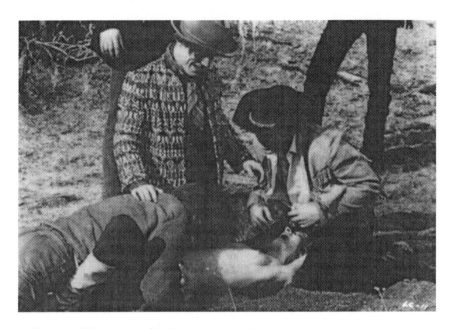

Ramona (Viva) is raped in *Lonesome Cowboys*.

another's misuse of mascara. The sheriff (Francis Francine) is a transvestite. To Parker Tyler, the film "derives logically from the emergence of the gay-cowboy charade as codified" in Howard Hughes's *The Outlaw*.[12] To George Cukor, "*Lonesome Cowboys* finishes the Western. I love the *swank* of it all – not bothering about details, the *dégagé* act of taking a Western street, not redressing it, letting tourists walk about in the background" and the self-satirizing plot: "When one of the brothers suddenly says, 'My parents were killed by Apaches, of course'? That 'of course' is brilliant, it's real satire."[13] There is a sobering gang rape of the Juliet character, Viva (as the virgin Ramona D'Alvarez), and seductive spasms by Taylor Mead (as Juliet's nurse). Perhaps the strongest moment is Viva's seduction of Tom Hompertz while chanting the Catholic benediction; however, this shocking scene lost some of its power when it was moved out of sequence to open the film.

Clearly the film touched a nerve. Though many reviewers proclaimed it *Warhol's* best film ever, when *Lonesome Cowboys* was screened in Atlanta (between runs of *Gone With the Wind* and Zeffirelli's – the other – *Romeo and Juliet*, as it happens) the print was seized for being, as the court solicitor's assistant put it, "obscene, vulgar and profane – just the type of thing that, in my opinion, would make the ordinary person sick."[14] When the audience was photographed so that their pictures could be compared with those of "known homosexuals," the American Civil Liberties Union sued for the destruction of the photos and to protest the unconstitutionality of the raid. The lesson Morrissey learned from this film is "not to burlesque the genre. It's better to keep a conventional structure and quietly plant the absurdities along the way." Fortunately, a helpful description of the rarely screened *Lonesome Cowboys* can be found in the FBI file on Warhol.[15]

For the record, Morrissey had nothing to do with *Andy Warhol's Bad* or his *Blue Movie* – even though both are commonly attributed to Warhol! Pat Hackett wrote the *Bad* screenplay for Morrissey. (Clue: in the opening scene Cyrinda Foxe stuffs a cafe toilet until it overflows.) After producer Robert Stigwood withdrew from the financing, Warhol still made it in 35 mm for $1 million. The film was directed on Morrissey's recommendation by his longtime assistant, Jed Johnson. Morrissey considers it "a good movie. Extremely irreverent, maybe a little too much so. It came out a little harsh. All the characters are terrible. Nobody's sympathetic. But Jed did a very good job, and it's undeniably funny." John Simon found the film "revolting in its misogyny."[16] After the commercial success of Morrissey's *Flesh,* when Warhol wanted to make a film with explicit sexual activity to regain his position on the front line, Morrissey set up the lighting for *Blue Movie,* using outdoor film for indoor shooting to give it a blue tint, but then left the set. Though the subject matter was repugnant to him, he defended the film when it was seized by the New York police, challenging them to define its difference from the unseized *I Am Curious (Yellow).*

In the beginning came *Flesh* (1969) – the first film formally attributed to Morrissey. The idea originated in a telephone conversation with Warhol, hospitalized from his near-fatal shooting by Valerie Solanis. Morrissey told Warhol that John Schlesinger was ignoring the entourage Morrissey had provided for the party scene in *Midnight Cowboy.*[17] Warhol suggested Morrissey make a film on the same subject, featuring the people Schlesinger left in the background. Morrissey filmed *Flesh* in some friends' apartments over five or six weekend afternoons for less than $3,000 (for the eight hours of film stock, developing, and printing). He edited it in his apartment on rewinds, without an editing table. He was still cutting it and adding the title card on Friday morning, then carried it to the theater for its Friday noon opening. It ran for a year in New York, grossing an average of $2,000 per week, despite its lack of a distributor. Morrissey himself handled the distribution in America. A major theatrical release in Germany, it proved among the top five box-office leaders, drawing three million viewers. It also proved a cause célèbre abroad.

In England, the police raided a *Flesh* screening on March 1, 1970, at Charles Marowitz's Open Space Club theater. In an unprecedented move, they arrested the entire audience. After the subsequent outcry, the police decided not to prosecute.[18] Later, *Trash* was refused an exhibition license because, although it provided an excoriating vision of the damage of hard drugs, it did not condemn the use of soft drugs.[19] Thirteen leading film critics wrote *The Times* of London deploring the delay in the licensing of *Trash* when such a violent film as Sam Peckinpah's *Straw Dogs* was quickly approved for public exhibition. These experiences did not alter Morrissey's conviction that "censorship is absolutely necessary. The English had the best idea: pick one intelligent person with common sense and who can see black and white, not some board. Fascists and liberals don't trust human beings so they trust committees." The British fiascoes, according to Morrissey, were the fault of the local boards' and the constabulary's "committee" mentality, not that of the British censor Trevelyan, whom Morrissey found to be "very reasonable." Ultimately *Flesh* and *Trash* were released uncut.

Now Morrissey was a filmmaker with an identifiable subject matter and style. To Warhol's nonnarrative cinema Morrissey introduced a quietly coherent succession of picaresque incidents that might be taken as plot; he also brought elements of technical sophistication, camera strategies, eruptions of black humor, and a penchant for letting his characters talk.

After *Flesh* and *Trash* came *Heat,* completing a trilogy that critiqued contemporary narcissism, respectively targeting sex, drugs, and the immoral media industry. Though *Heat* had the technique and style of a mainstream Hollywood film, even it was made in two weeks, without a script, on a budget of less than $15,000; this included travel to California, motel rental, and the "large" star fee of $5,000 to the redoubtable Sylvia Miles, fresh from her Oscar nomination for *Midnight Cowboy. Heat* was the first Warhol production screened at the Venice Film Festival. After his most comic film, *Women in Revolt,* Morrissey expanded his range with two pointed costume potboilers, his Frankenstein and Dracula larks. These two films formally ended Morrissey's association with the Factory, as he stayed on in Europe, then moved to Los Angeles, feeling the need to be independent beyond even the autonomy Warhol gave him.

Despite Morrissey's puritanism, the success of his *Flesh* trilogy and his horror films was at least in part due to the films' sexual openness – or at least the promise of such. He says, "We always had to wave some sensational title to get people into the theater because the critics wouldn't help us at all."[20] As it happens, the films are far from the porn they may have been hoped – or hyped – to be. Explicit for their time, now they seem merely suggestive, to the point that Morrissey has even been charged with "Hollywood's prurient self-censorship."[21]

In fact, the films constitute a critique of the very business of exploitation films and the general commodification of the human being. Morrissey rejects the false allure of contemporary freedoms because they reduce people into manipulable, salable commodities. As David James observes, *Flesh* and *Trash* "affront commercial expectations as much by retarding the narrative in prolonged visual scrutiny of their stars as by their salacious subject matter."[22] But even as Morrissey took pains to violate the slick look of commercial films, he flouted the ethos of the exploitation film. His libertines are pathetic. There is no gratification in the urgency and futility that Morrissey's films portray. This makes their uncommercial look not just a matter of economy but of principle: from *Flesh* through *Spike of Bensonhurst* (and one expects, beyond), Morrissey's target is the commodification of the human being, whether the human sale is a matter of sexual prostitution, the buying of a boxer or a great musician's vampirish hold on his nephew. This ethic is paralleled by Morrissey's insistence upon staying outside of the commodity cinema. He has never used an agent to "package" one of his films.

He even steers clear of the commercial when he makes such popular successes as his *Dracula* and *Frankenstein* comic horrors. Both films were shot in a total of seven weeks, without a finished script. Morrissey suggested the dialogue and plot turns on a day-to-day basis. "I think the secretary [Pat Hackett, who typed up the daily plot addition] made up most of the dialogue," Morrissey told an AFI audience.[23] The actors got their lines in the morning and learned them during the lighting setup. "Each night I'd think of what further absurdity might logically follow from where I began," Morrissey says. Originally only the *Frankenstein* was planned. Then producer Carlo Ponti suggested that while everyone was together they may as well make another film. "So we finished *Frankenstein* one morning, broke for lunch, a couple of the cast had haircuts, then we started *Dracula* in the afternoon." Even under such conditions, Morrissey does not merely exercise the genre conventions. He turns them to serve his personal concern with powerful people living off the weak. His comic irony and extravagance further distance him from the apparatus of the commercial cinema.

Morrissey continues to work with low budgets, on principle as much as of necessity. His experimental play recording, *Forty-Deuce,* cost only $150,000 but was an official selection at Cannes. A squabble over distribution rights has the film out of circulation, except for its release in Australia and Europe, and a French-subtitled print available in Quebec. His extremely polished *Mixed Blood* cost only $400,000, although it was filmed in 35 mm. *Beethoven's Nephew* and *Spike of Bensonhurst* cost $1 million and $3 million respectively, astonishingly small budgets for such polished works.

Whenever possible, Morrissey tries to work without unions. While he appreciates their expertise, it has its costs. He had to shoot *Spike of Bensonhurst* in Greenpoint, Brooklyn, because he couldn't afford the union expenses of driving out to Bensonhurst. He says,

> The whole union thing is perpetrated by people who are insecure. They want to obscure their lack of content, plot, and the most important thing, characters. So you get enormous photography and technical polish but there's nothing going on in characterization. They just want to make the film look good. But the story and the people will carry the day so I leave the camera on the people. I can't change that.

Yet, Morrissey respects directors like Ophuls and Visconti whose opulence and technique always serve their characterization and themes.

Morrissey's career shows two unsuccessful tangents. One was a period comedy, *Hound of the Baskervilles*, "the only film I ever made reluctantly. I wasn't confident in it. I saw it as a possible companion piece to the preceding two costume films, all based on famous legends. However, I lost control over it at the very beginning when it was suggested that the two main actors (Peter Cook and Dudley Moore) each write a section of the film." This was an attempt to resurrect the music hall tradition of British comedy against the more cerebral and surrealist "wise guy university humor" of Beyond the Fringe and the later Monty Python's Flying Circus. Morrissey recruited such comic stalwarts as Irene Handl, Max Wall, and Spike Milligan. But the film is an uneasy pastiche. It swerves between the brash humor of Peter Cook and Dudley Moore – as in Sherlock Holmes's (Cook's) interview with a one-legged man (Moore) who wants a job as his runner – and the Carry On Gang's rather single-minded *double entendre*, as in this fruity remembrance of a character washed overboard during a storm at sea:

TERRY-THOMAS: Did you manage to drag yourself up on deck?
KENNETH WILLIAMS: No, I dressed rather casual.

Gratuitous parodies, most indigestibly of *The Exorcist,* compound the incoherence. As Morrissey, Cook, and Moore wrote their parts separately, the film never did come together. Moore and Cook seemed more proficient at improvising sketches than at developing a full feature. From "the only film I wasn't in total control of," nothing of his interests can be fairly inferred – except, perhaps, from Denholm Elliot's dog urinating into Dudley Moore's face.

Morrissey's other detour was directing a Broadway musical, *The Man in the Moon,* which closed after a few days at the Little Theatre on West 44th Street in January 1975. This was a family entertainment space musical produced two years before *Star Wars* would have made it fashionable. The Nemo-like plot had a German scientist, angry that the U.S. government had cut off his space funding, send a dim astronaut to the moon: he gets lost. The play was unusual in that it didn't have any Broadway dance numbers, just eighteen John Phillips songs, of which at least fifteen advanced the plot, Morrissey recalls. And there was no rock and roll in the show. Monique Van Vooren was the only Broadway veteran in the cast. Morrissey had cowriting problems with the song team of star Genevieve Waite and husband John Phillips.

Apart from these two tangents, Morrissey's canon is an impressive series of artistic experiment and success with a single moral vision behind it. However off the wall Morrissey's characters and plot, or on the mark their wall-to-wall chatter, one ethic propels the Morrissey cinema: "I want to remark upon the waste of life." And nothing wastes human life more than a weakling's self-indulgence and the exploitation of it. As the commercial cinema perpetuates the view that film is a product, it confirms the unscrupulous assumption that people are products, whether as consumers of the film or as exploitable merchandise themselves. "The three dominant religions that are fashionably worshipped today – sex, drugs, and rock and roll – are, I think, inherently evil and destructive to life. The dehumanization caused by these stupid, selfish, schlock incitements to license have brought people to hate themselves, their countries, their families, and their life. It's a very serious problem that demands to be treated comically, as it is a self-imposed insanity, brainwashed into the general population by the media's nonstop efforts to pander to uneducated children and semiliterate adults."

Instead of the calculated coldness of Warhol's obsessive gaze, Morrissey cares for the unpromising characters he reveals. In Warhol's fascination merely to watch, suppressing all emotional or intellectual response, he rediscovered film's mechanical power simply to register reality. Not content with Warhol's mechanical, passive stare, Morrissey is compelled to feel – and to make his viewers feel – for the human ruins in his focus. Because of his involvement in his characters, Morrissey avoids both the objective recording of their pathetic existence and any explicit attack on them. His films implicitly critique the drugged world for its false glamour and mortal waste. Far from glorifying their characters' modish freedom, the films expose the tragedy of their destructive self-abuse, the emptiness of the total freedom encouraged by a merchandise-dominated world. But because Morrissey cares for his creatures he refrains from explicit criticism, preferring their own words to reveal and to frame them. So his films emerge as implicit critiques, free of the hectoring moralist. For George Cukor, "The selection of people, the casting, is absolutely brilliant and impertinent.... I've never seen any documentaries or any 'low life' studies that have a grain of humor. They're usually soggy, or they have that deadly touch of the schoolmaster. ... Nobody has any kind of guilt in [the Warhol/Morrissey] pictures. None of the attitudes are conventional, you never see a tear – that's extremely refreshing!"[24] Morrissey's trenchant ironies invite the ambivalent response of a hard judgment – but one that is profoundly caring. The respectful free rein he gives his remarkable performers keeps the films comedies.

In both his morality and his aesthetic, Morrissey's films attack the commodification in commercial film. They are distinguished by precisely what Koch complains about, for Morrissey rejects "Warhol's Duchampian dehumanization of the cinematic eye" and Warhol's "inattentive camera."[25] In Parker Tyler's words, "The Warholist film camera is the catatonic film camera: the camera that literally *does least* for whatever it photographs." Warhol's "pseudoaesthetic strategy" was to play possum, or "chameleon, protecting himself by remaining perfectly still and relying on his environment to efface him."[26] But Morrissey resists his offensive environment. To assert his opposition, he prefers art that serves life, the art of a feeling humanity that transcends the mechanical. Morrissey's cool satire is compassionate: "Every movie I've made, the main characters have been unbelievably foolish – that's how I get to like them.... When I see their failings and their vulnerability, I know there's a character there."[27]

Paradoxically, this puts Morrissey outside the modern movements of abstract art and the experimental cinema and inside the humanist tradition of Jean Renoir and Robert Bresson, with whose films the feel and look of a Morrissey film have absolutely nothing in common. But then, Paul Morrissey has always been independent of the independents, outside the outsiders. The Carol Reed acolyte is an Odd Man Out himself, an outcast from all the islands.

2
The *Flesh* Trilogy

Morrissey broke out of the Warhol shadow with a surprisingly successful trilogy of films that he wrote, photographed, and directed with minimal resources from 1968 to 1972. Although all three films carry Warhol's title (*Andy Warhol Presents Flesh*, etc.) they are clearly Morrissey's films. True, they retain elements of what is usually considered the "Warhol aesthetic." This Morrissey has called "exaggerated naturalism": unconventional acting, lack of scripting, minimal camera work, the visible economy of verisimilitude, and a focus on the life-styles of the libertine and lethargic. But even where the films cohere with the Warhol aesthetic, they follow what he and Morrissey had done together, not Warhol's pre-Morrissey films, which were minimalist provocations with a single camera position. The more successful aesthetic evolved during Morrissey's control of the Factory experiments.

The trilogy also contributed to the period's revolutionary openness in its new explicitness in images both of drug use and of sexuality. After all, *Hair* – with its nude be-in – opened on Broadway in April 1968, and the even bawdier *Oh, Calcutta!* opened in June 1969. In film, Morrissey opened a new frontier in the representation of male nudity. There are more dangling penises in this trilogy than you can shake a stick at. Simply in depicting the male hustler's life in *Flesh*, Morrissey extended the boundaries of American cinema.[1] Even in their adaptation of Warren Miller's *The Cool World* (1963), Shirley Clarke and Frederick Wiseman omitted the gay prostitute, Chester (though Clarke later confronted the character type's speech, if not deeds, in her *Portrait of Jason*). Rather new for the uptown cinemas was a film in which the camera leered at the naked male with the open fascination traditionally spent solely upon the female. "No one had yet done it, and we had to be different," Morrissey says. Morrissey continued Warhol's compulsion (from his art-school cause célèbre of the nose-picking self-portrait on) to show the forbidden, to batter down the taboos, but without his mentor's evasiveness. Without showing any hard-core specifics, Morrissey's *Trash* opens with a much clearer and more explicit "blow job" than the famous Warhol film of that name and subject.

Despite these extensions of "the Warhol cinema," Morrissey's films broke away in several key respects. Technically, Morrissey adopted plot, characterization, more controlled sound and color, the impulse to expressive camera and editing work, and working professionals. Morrissey's technical advances always had a purpose, however, or at least a telling effect. For example, a panning camera across even a static space would emphasize the distance between his characters. In the last shot of *Trash*, the space between the lovers expresses their unbridgeable alienation, after their separate close-ups and the woman's offer of union. The stricter the style, the more meaningful is the slightest nuance.

With these strategies Morrissey built upon what he considered Warhol's major discovery: "People themselves are the information," he says. "The content is so interesting – it should be. You don't have to emphasize it with dramatic notions." Dramatic structuring and dramatic acting styles are to him old-fashioned:

> Today a lot of things are very banal and very prosaic and very casual, no standards, much has no strict morality. Everything is a bit easy-going. If you tell a modern story, you're better off with this casualness. ...There are very few stories about modern life on the screen. The techniques for telling those stories, I think, are different than the techniques for telling stories where there was a moral or there was a standard...of life. Techniques change with life.[2]

Morrissey's unobtrusive aesthetic points to his ethic, that is, quietly to expose the emptiness of contemporary liberty. Instead of railing, Morrissey lets his viewer dig out the import of his pretended indifference and humor.

To the alerted eye, often what seems to be a casual shot explodes in aptness and meaning. For example, in *Trash*, when Joe fumbles in close-up trying to find his vein for the needle, we expect the camera to pan away discreetly, perhaps to some subtle and more assuring tradition (read: cliché), such as fireworks or the Moscow fountains. Instead, Morrissey keeps in the film his camera's gradual focusing. By refusing to interrupt the moment he is recording, he claims veracity. He also provides a process of focusing that acts against the viewer's impulse to turn away from the disturbing but fascinating image. The architect tells *us* as well as his wife to watch Joe shooting up, when he punctuates her chatter with exhortations to *look:*

"Watch this, my dear. It's your performance.... Pay attention.... Would you look!... Jane, look!... Will you look at what's happening!... Look. Look.... Would you watch this!" The content of that shot, then, is not just the needle entering the flesh or even our seeing that happen, but our having our attention focused on the incident, in mixed fascination and repugnance. Morrissey then cuts seamlessly from the close-ups on Joe to a dramatic God's-eye-view, when Joe overdoses. The down-shot freezes Joe like a specimen against the couple's superiority, imaged in the oriental carpet on which he's pinned by the camera; the angle situates us at a superior height. Although he mistakenly attributes this effect to Warhol instead of to Morrissey, David James's elaboration on this point is shrewd: "His is thus a meta-cinema, an inquiry into the mechanisms of the inscription of the individual into the apparatus and into the way such inscription has been historically organized. In it the spectator is revealed as being as much a function of the camera as are the actors."[3]

The focusing needle shot also reinforces the film's theme of voyeurism, of Joe's reduction to object of (among other things) visual exploitation. That a Factory film might indeed develop themes constitutes a radical departure from the Warhol aesthetic. The theme of the drug addict's objectification (or voyeurist exploitation) was introduced in the Andrea Feldman character: "I want to see you shoot up.... I *love* to watch this." On a close-up of Joe piercing his vein she says, "The only kind of man I want is real men." For his part, Joe is given several key close-ups that define him as a pathetic, helpless witness to his replacement in his partner Holly's needs (by a young John, for example, and by a beer bottle). Usually the object of others' uses, Joe is himself reduced by his drugs to being able only to watch others do what he no longer can.

At other times, the vacancy in the performer, the tightness in the framing and the articulated vacuity of the character combine into compelling cinema. The down-shot on Joe's overdosing takes on another level of absurdist inspiration from the yuppie wife's (Jane Forth's) jabbering about cosmetics in a marriage that is cosmetic, and in a cosmetic craving for the freakish: "Did you know that egg yolks on your skin makes you look Oriental?" she says.

For these obvious advances Morrissey was branded a commercial sellout in the Factory, as the recent spate of Warhol reminiscences consistently attest. Warhol's private view was that "Paul was nuts... he really believes all these wild theories he comes up with."[4] (There's a distinction for you: to have one's ideas called nuts by Andy Warhol.) But these very "compromises" have given the Morrissey films a longevity and interest long after

Warhol's "purer" experiments have faded into either the archive or the oblivion of the rare museum retrospective. More to the point, far from being a matter of commercial compromise, *Flesh* launched Morrissey's war against the modern tendency to turn everything – people as well as art and films – into merchandisable commodities.

Flesh (1968)

The opening shot in Morrissey's first independent feature seems to raise the Warhol shadow in order for Morrissey to detach himself from it. A two-and-a-half minute close-up on a sleeping Joe Dallesandro evokes Warhol's most notorious feature, the six-hour silent *Sleep* (1963). "In contrast to [Warhol's] abstracted details of male anatomy," David Bourdon suggests, "*Flesh* presents Dallesandro's nude body in its entirety."[5] Further, Morrissey enriches his rhetoric with detail. Joe lies on a blanket patterned with gaping teeth, like the *vagina dentata,* implying an anxiety of emasculation. On the soundtrack, a zippy old song (supposedly on the television), invites "whoo-pee makers" and "wide awakers" to the joys of "Making wicky wacky down in Waikiki." The ensuing feature uses Village whoopee makers to question how wide awake and self-aware such benighted narcissists may be.

Both the themes of sleeping consciousness and narcissism continue in the second shot, a full rear view of Dallesandro's sleeping body. From here on – indeed through the entire trilogy – Morrissey implicitly explores his hero's pride (including his converse self-destruction in *Trash*), his indulgence in his own body, and his audience's fascination with the naked male form. In all three films Dallesandro remains only the attractive "shell" of a hero, with none of the values or character strength that his appearance may promise.

The film ends as it began, but with a difference. Again Dallesandro is naked on his belly in bed. Reversing the opening order, the full-length view is followed by the profile close-up. But now Joe is no longer alone. His wife Geraldine (Geraldine Smith) is asleep beside him, but between them lies her new lover, Patti (Patti d'Arbanville), the women's legs ardently intertwined. We see him in the relationship from which he is excluded. Joe's naked solitude is redefined as an alienation within a relationship. Both the opening and the closing pose the Dallesandro character in passivity.[6] As the film begins and ends with Joe in bed, the narrative is given a circular frame, reminding us that life is rounded off with a sleep and a forgetting. The closing circle also suggests a permanent noncommitment: there is little difference between Joe's waking and sleeping states.

Joe is roused from his initial sleep by his scolding wife, who nags him to go to work to raise the $200 that Patti needs for a (later abandoned) abortion. Although her scolding and violence give way to her erotic play, it in turn is aborted by Joe's less romantic concerns: "Do my laundry, will you? Without me asking? Just once?.... You really want to make me happy? Do my laundry." Though it is amusing to find such traditional domestica in bohemia, the point runs deeper than satire. As Margaret Tarratt observed, "Much of the film's strength comes from its close observation of people and their contradictory impulses between brashness and uncertainty, openness and evasiveness, desire and avarice."[7] The scene ends with Geraldine wrapping up Joe's penis in a white ribbon. This comic gift wrapping introduces Joe's commodification: Geraldine packages Joe's sexuality and deploys it for her lover Patti's needs.

After this ribald opening, there is an eloquent domestic coda. In a completely silent three-minute montage, the naked Joe plays with his baby, feeding him crumbs of cupcake, then stands dressed while Geraldine silently irons Joe's white shirt. The silence sets off the tenderness of the entire scene. It also emphasizes the softness of the baby's flesh and the natural warmth of the naked father at ease with his child. Such warmth and intimacy Joe will not again experience in the film. As well, the scene establishes something childlike in Joe. He and the baby seem able to take their pleasure in the moment, as simple nibbles of appetite without weighty import or compulsiveness. It's a scene of appetite without hunger; it suggests sustenance instead of dissipation. This scene contrasts Joe's sexual exploitation; the pragmatic identity he later teaches the neophyte hustlers seems here a childlike purity.

We follow Joe through a variety of subtly demeaning encounters. On the level of plot, they enable him to raise the $200 he has promised Geraldine. On the level of theme, they play variations on the compromise of self-respect by sexual commodification. As Joe tells his wife, his professional sexual liberty is "very painful. I don't like that kind of work." From the quiet intimacy with his baby, Joe goes out to sell himself on the cacophonous street. *Flesh* draws less on the sentimental treatment of the subject in *Midnight Cowboy* than on Warhol's *My Hustler* (1965), where a self-absorbed stud remains the empty object of other people's fantasies and desires.

In a wordless five-minute montage of street life, Joe waits and watches and displays himself to watchers. In the first shot he is reflected in a street puddle, as if he were greasy rubble (anticipating the central metaphor of the subsequent *Trash*). The main point is that we see the variety of ways in which Joe is being watched. Indeed our watching him becomes predatory when we strain to find his small figure in the teeming street life. The watching ends in use (that is, he turns from object of vision to sexual object); he turns his first trick in a toilet for $20 (it's an old movie). The deal is straightforward, except for the two men's ritual hope to meet again ("I'll be seeing you soon").

The emptiness of such expressions is made clearer through Joe's two major clients that day. Neither admits the meaning of his interest in Joe. Both idealize their interest – and Morrissey accepts their positions. Joe's second customer (Maurice Braddell) articulates Morrissey's concern, saying, "Best to give you pride in your job, your vocation." But this client's "pride" is a matter of mutual delusion: the British gentleman veils his homosexuality in aestheticism. He poses Joe nude in order to photograph and then draw him. In David James's view, this is "an especially articulate version of such scenarios of scopophilia, in which the spectator's, the camera's, and the performer's gazes coincide upon his body. Reduced to an object of visual consumption, he enacts this function both *in* the film and *for* the film. . . . Dallesandro's dramatic situation restates the use the film makes of him. . . . In the economics of spectatorship, each of us is the industry's John and Braddell our proxy."[8]

The aging aesthete further rationalizes his proclivity by citing the Greeks' drawing of "empathy" and "sympatico" (the feelings as well as the words) from their erotic sculpture and by positing a religion of sensuality:

In a liberated person . . . body worship is behind all art, all music, and all sex and all love. If you cut it out for any reason you've deprived yourself of one whole chunk of life. . . . Body worship is in – is *in* the makeup of the human animal. All human beings, whether they're Puritanicals or whatever they are, they like it. . . . [From art and movies] they all get what they call the sex kick, which is bullshit. There's no sex in it. It's body worship, which becomes sex.

The heartiness of the man's philosophy is undermined by his ascetic image and his reedy voice.

And yet . . . and yet something of the gentleman's pretension still speaks for Morrissey. Morrissey often casts performers of idealized appearance because

good looks are one of the few visible elements in contemporary life that remind us of the past, when life had some meaning. This was the case with the Greeks, with the Renaissance, with the nineteenth century and even with Hollywood of the thirties and forties. Physical beauty suggested the dignity and worthiness of human life. Juxtaposing a former ideal with today's sordid reality gives the work a tension and dramatic conflict. To me, just to survive this stupidity makes the central figure some kind of hero. None of my modern heroes have any big ambitions or aspirations. Just enough job or money to subsist on. None of my contemporary characters is ever so naive as to expect or to want "love" or even any kind of affection. They live in a world where things like that are long gone, dead, and they know it. Of course, this has alienated the liberal critics who want to see the old clichés of love and sex as "the meaning of life." They want to believe, they have to believe, that love can still exist in a sexually free society. Because they have destroyed the potential for affection in reality, they have to have it, if only in fantasy.

The aesthete's rationalization is paralleled by Joe's last customer of the day, the macho younger man (Louis Waldon) whom Joe knows from the gyms. He pretends that their sex is for friendlier motive than the money Joe always requests and that despite their sex, "we're not queers." The pretense to friendship is undermined when the customer shifts from jocular suggestion to brusquely ordering Joe about. The client's delusions show his need for purity in a relationship – such as that glimpsed in Joe's scene with the baby, but impossible for him elsewhere because of the commercialization of intimacy. Only with the baby is Joe in a relationship in which he is not a commodity.

In Gene Youngblood's view, *Flesh* "epitomizes the unisex world of The Factory. The Brandoesque Joe Dallesandro is virtually the embodiment of polymorphous perverse man as Morrissey interprets him: the archetypal erotic body, responding to the pleasures of the flesh without ideals or violence in a pansexual universe."[9] But Youngblood overlooks Morrissey's sense of the emptiness of Joe's life. Joe's bisexuality may well represent a recovery of infantile bisexuality, a presocial (or in the repressed and repressive American society, antisocial) natural drive. But Joe's sexual openness can only be partial once he leaves his home. Outside it is delimited and redefined by the capitalism that commodifies everything, especially sexuality and freedom. The result of Joe's radical sexual freedom, then, is that he is bought and enslaved for it. Freedom to be bought is a dubious freedom.

The liberty of Joe's bisexuality is exposed as debilitating when, unfettered and commercialized, it exposes all the other hollow characters. Geraldine's bisexuality and the baby–man scene both evoke Freud's denial of a clear distinction between the masculine and the feminine natures. As Joe becomes a specular object, he assumes the traditional female role, while the more aggressive women in his life – Geraldine, Geri – adopt a more masculine character. This gender cross is literalized in the transvestites, whose transcendence of their biological gender proves a remarkable will and integrity.

Between the two commercialized male unions, with their self- and mutual deception, Joe finds more honesty in two other groups. In the first he discusses his trade with two would-be hustlers from Wisconsin. His theme is that it doesn't matter what people think of each other in this commercial exchange of flesh. Further, "Nobody's straight. What's straight? It's not a matter of being straight, being not straight. It's just – you just do what you have to do." Joe is touching in his willingness to teach the younger men, to soften their initiation into a hard, brutal life.

In the second group, Morrissey pans between two drag queens (Jackie Curtis and Candy Darling) reading a Hollywood fan magazine and Joe getting a blow job from an old girlfriend, Geri (Geri Miller). Like the opening detachment from *Sleep,* this scene seems determined to provide a social and psychological context to the act that is only implied in Warhol's famous forty-five minute film, *Blow Job* (1964), which has been called "the longest 'reaction shot' on record."[10] David Bourdon declares Morrissey's blow job "more naturalistic, explicit and physical" than Warhol's, and thereto played "for raunchy laughs."[11] One comic frisson derives from the incongruity of such a private act performed before two witnesses. Because the two groups are in the same room but never in the same frame, they seem isolated within company (like Joe on his ménage à trois marriage bed). Alternatively, the pan speaks to the fact that, as eroticism resides in the head, what else happens in the same room is irrelevant. Another irony derives from the transvestites' glamour-ad quotations. For example, one – "When is a tampon right for you?" – directly confronts the commercialization of sexual identity, all the more ironic for a transvestite. Other lines allude to the sexual activity from which the reading is supposedly a distraction: "Jergens face cream," "battle of the bulge." Further, as David James suggests, "Orally consumed by Miller, Dallesandro is visually consumed by Curtis and Darling. With his back to the camera he looks away from everyone, . . . as in the twin-screen projections, one scene is in competition with the other, the exchange of glances passing from screen to screen, from the image of the subject of visual consumption to the image of the object of visual consumption, a doubled relay which dramatizes the real and the fantasy roles within spectatorship."[12] The transvestites are both charming and dignified, especially when they urge

Candy Darling, Joe Dallesandro, and Geri Miller discuss Geri's plans for a silicone implant in *Flesh*.

Geri not to get silicone enlargements of her breasts, envying her natural femininity: "Things that move are beautiful. Like your bust. It moves."

For all her naïveté, Geri is distinguished by two instances of self-knowledge. In one, she accepts her mental limitations without pretensions: "My brain can't be developed any more than it is. And I think I'm cute. I don't want to change. If I learn too much I won't be happy. I think the more you learn the more depressed you are." Her self-acceptance contrasts Joe's two male clients, who both have art collections and claim to "illuminate" Joe. Geri also establishes a dramatic integrity when she explains to Joe how she avenged herself for a gang rape, when she was coerced under threat. She saw her rapists again when she was dancing at a club:

> Do you know what it's like to be topless in front of someone who raped you? And that was how I got him back. Cause, like, he didn't think I'd have the guts to dance in front of him. And I just danced the best I could, to say "This is what you didn't get." Cause, like, when he raped me I was real stiff.... Because he just took it I was real awful. And that's how much I love you. I didn't want to let them hurt you.

Throughout this astonishing disclosure, Geri and Joe are in tight close-up, but Geri faces the camera full while Joe stands in profile, detached and smoking. Joe seems unmoved by her powerful story. She explains that Joe left her when she denied him after the trauma of the rape. Later she does her topless dance at Joe's request but he ignores her. Amid the triviality and falsity of Joe's sexual deals, Geri is his most honest – and therefore undervalued – engagement.

Geri's generous but abused love for Joe also contrasts his wife's exploitation of him. Over his protests, Geraldine and Patti undress Joe. They berate him for his laziness and chatter over his attempts to sleep. Finally, Patti clambers over him to embrace his wife. When Joe rises to watch his sleeping wife and her lover he may finally be awakening to the fact that he is literally spending himself for a relationship of only partial commitment. But he stays a sleepwalker, as he watches placidly, without Geri's resolve to reaffirm her own self-respect. The narcissistic Joe, his name and nature tattooed on his flesh as if that were his sole significance, remains isolated in the sensual shallows of flesh worship.

Joe's flickering consciousness may well be imaged in one idiosyncrasy in the film's technique, a jerkiness in the editing within a shot and in the frequent elision in dialogue. Often a character's speech is cut off before a sentence ends, or a single word or phrase may seem removed. These deliberate devices suggest characters stoned and screwed into a strobelike discontinuity of perception and understanding.

Morrissey's human touches in *Flesh* were not universally accepted. Greg Ford dismissed Joe's scene with the baby as an "interminable affair... the only occasion at which imputations of 'sentimentality' or 'mawkishness' could correctly be pegged on a Factory picture." He found the street montage "self-conscious virtuosity."[3] Although Jonas Mekas claimed the film "has no special aesthetic or stylistic values" he still declared it "a good illustration of what Andy Warhol isn't about.... a Warhol film never gives you an impression that it wants to make itself interesting."[4] This is damning with apt praise. In contrast, John Weightman acknowledged the "very powerful and beautiful effect" when Joe's scene with the baby reverses the neoclassical genre painting in which the adult remained clothed and the child nude. "The nakedness of the father seemed to suggest that human beings are children who beget other children and can only look at them with puzzled affection, without understanding what the whole process is about."[5]

Such, precisely, is the mystery of the – as the title should alert us – *flesh*, to the one creature who can think and/or make art about it. Morrissey is rare for having thought about the flesh as well as showing it. The basic subject of the film is flesh. It is our glory or our failing. The staff of potency dangles pathetically, ludicrous in a ribbon, because our flesh is both our peak and our base. Those who have it handsomely will be bought and sold for it. Even if they are violently craved, those who think themselves inadequate will have silicone augmentation. Those who feel they have the wrong flesh will project a persona that flies in the face of their native flesh. The baby flesh will thoughtlessly nibble a crumbling cake. At the other end of life, the crumbling old man will buy some younger flesh and rationalize his interest, to fend off his shame if not time. Between them, the young and innocent aspire to sell theirs. The older rake who will buy them worries about a wound, his flesh scarred by experience, and hits the gyms to avert flab. This man will squeeze a pimple on his lover's face because he needs another man's perfection to assure him against the loss of his own. Fidelity calls for the sacrifice of one flesh to preserve the integrity of another. So the stripper acknowledges shame but transcends it for her self, as earlier she yielded her flesh to protect her lover. He in turn peddles his flesh so his fleshmate can abort the new flesh growing in her lover's womb. These ripe paradoxes suggest a human and social contract written entirely in the flesh and its uses. To be blessed with being is to be cursed with flesh. Though – or because? – it is what we essentially are, to dedicate ourselves to it is folly.

Trash (1970)

As the title suggests, Morrissey's second film deals with the range of "trash" in his street-life survey. The original title, *Drug Trash,* pointed to Morrissey's intended target as the patrons of the "Swillmore Vomitorium,"[16] who were turning subhuman by deadening themselves with drugs. Morrissey considered them worse than the Bowery winos because they self-righteously disguised their weakness as championing liberty. The film's realism dispelled the myth "that drugs are supposed to free people from inhibitions."[17] Morrissey wanted to counteract the romanticizing of drug use in *Easy Rider* and in the perception of the "ultimate trip" of *2001: A Space Odyssey.* "The basic idea for the movie," he says, "is that drug people are trash. There's no difference between a person using drugs and a piece of refuse."[18]

But the film expresses a broader, more forgiving humanity than Morrissey suggests. It's yet another proof that – in D. H. Lawrence's injunction – we should trust the art, not the artist. The shorter title permits a broader reading

39

of the film: it's also about people being inappropriately treated as trash and also about the need to recover the ruins among us, whether thrown-away furniture or discarded people.

Perhaps the film's shift to a more compassionate breadth derived from Morrissey's discovery of Holly Woodlawn, erstwhile transvestite and female impersonator Harold Danhaki. With her animated face and bravado, Holly dominates the film, defines its moral and emotional center, and commands our identification. Holly's spirit, will, and zany charm make this potentially depressing drama an uplifting comedy.

Morrissey had not met Woodlawn before she started to play the lead role in *Trash*. He read an interview in which Woodlawn claimed to be one of Warhol's Superstars; in fact, the two had never even met. Impressed by Holly's spirit, he invited her to the filming.

> She came over Saturday at one to the basement in my house, where I was going to shoot. I told her: Joe looks for junk to shoot and you look for junk in the streets and you're both junk. So I shot a reel and looked at it on Tuesday and she was great. So now I knew my movie. It was going to be about *her* and Joe. And I just met her on the set and she'd never been in a movie before.

With the advent of Holly, the film seems to have shifted from being about the trash who use drugs to people determined to salvage a discarded humanity.

As Marsha Kinder and Beverle Houston point out, the order of the episodes enhances and validates the Holly–Joe relationship that we see in five of the eight sequences. The welfare scenes "are particularly strong in destroying stereotypes and revealing subtly the tenderness, loyalty and complexity of their relationship." Joe's first and last scenes with Holly "are the only two scenes in the film between people who have no hostility toward each other."[9] If the film was conceived as an exposé of the drug trash, it became the touching story of the woman striving to salvage ruined lives. Perhaps Morrissey framed the film with music from von Sternberg's *The Blue Angel* (1930) to point up a curious plot reversal: Holly replaces the elderly professor who wastes his life in devotion to a worthless icon (Joe standing in for Marlene Dietrich). Alternatively, as Kinder and Houston suggest, the allusion implies the films' common "affirmation of the beauty and pathos of human degradation."[20]

This broader spirit makes for a more engaging film. At the time, Morrissey described the film as "decadent fluff, but realistic. . . . I'm really for social criticism through entertainment. New York people are too hard-boiled to regard messages as very important."[21] Though topical, the film has hardly dated after twenty years. Morrissey thought that the drug scene was just a passing fad, but "to my surprise, all the basically trashy ideas of the sixties went on to become the established ideas of the eighties, and they're still in power."

In his typically insightful review, John Weightman described this black comedy's universe: "This is total abjection, not simply man without God or man alienated from society, but Beckettian man in the dust-bin waiting for death."[22] Joe (Dallesandro) and Holly Santiago (Holly Woodlawn) live in an unheated basement that they furnish with trash that Holly scrounges from the street. Holly takes her trash seriously. As she warns Joe when he roughly moves their unfixed pedestal sink, "Careful. People gonna pee in there." From the outside perspective, the characters themselves are trash, like the refuse they drag in from the streets.

But the couple is enhanced by their contrast to the ostensibly superior uptown folks who pass through their orbit. The latter seem uniformly idle. Both the rich girl (Andrea Feldman) and the topless dancer (Geri Miller) cite television as attractive diversion. Feldman plays the first of the "respectable" characters, as she asks Joe for LSD. Then a high school kid (Johnny Putnam) comes to Holly for dope. When Joe tries to burgle an upscale apartment, he encounters a handsome young newlywed couple, Bruce and Jane (Bruce Pecheur and Jane Forth, a sixteen-year-old last-minute replacement for Patti d'Arbanville). Fascinated by the lurid, they watch him shoot up, then quarrel. When Joe appears to have dangerously overdosed, they throw him out naked and cold into the hallway, where they normally put their trash. Jane's reservation is strictly formal: "Is this the way to treat a guest in my house?" she asks. Joe becomes another used, then discarded commodity. These characters establish the folly of drug use across class and economic lines. Joe's poverty makes his debility all the more visible. Both wealthy women goad Joe into futile rape attempts, from their own jadedness, in contrast to Geri's and Holly's emotional need for Joe's resurrected loving. After Holly rails at him, Joe passes out; she then reaches into his pants and pathetically asks, "Why do you have to be unconscious?" Her plaint refers to his drugged waking state as much as to the moment.

In two wholly improvised scenes, Holly articulates a dignity and self-respect that deny her identification as trash. When she finds Joe in bed with her pregnant sister (Diane Podlewski), Holly rails at her betrayal by her two dearest people. In Woodlawn's marvelous improvisation, as Kinder and Houston note, her original emotions of sexual jealousy and indignation soften under her maternal sentiments: "There's her mattress, now she's never

41

Holly Woodlawn negotiates with the social worker (Michael Sklar) in *Trash*.

going to use it. And her kid's bassinet – so what if it's only a drawer."[23]
Her integrity is confirmed later, when she refuses the offer of Mr. Michaels
(Michael Sklar),[24] the social worker, to give her welfare support in exchange
for the silver platform shoes she found in the garbage. Wanting to make a
faddish lamp out of them, and with his use of "groovy" and his nuclear
disarmament button, Mr. Michaels personifies Morrissey's dread "liberal."
By resisting the social worker's (and Joe's) pressure, Holly refuses to be
exploited. In both cases, trash that only Holly has seen fit to salvage (Joe,
the shoes) suddenly becomes valued by others, and she may lose them. The
implication is that she alone has stable values, while others operate by whim.

Both scenes imperil the couple's scheme to claim Holly's sister's baby as
theirs, in order to get welfare. (This ploy is revived by a minor character
buying drugs in the 1984 *Mixed Blood*.) "I wanted to try to get back on
welfare. Be respectable," Holly says ruefully. "I need welfare. I deserve
it. ... Now I'll feel like a piece of garbage. Welfare won't take me." The
loss of welfare hurts Holly because she craves domestic stability and
respectability.

Woodlawn was aware of a double emotion in her role: "I wanted to look

42

ridiculous and to make people laugh. But I also wanted them to *feel* something for me, to *feel* something for that pitiful girl with no future."[25] Holly's spontaneous disclosure that her father "minces vegetables" at Blimpy's for a living is an example of what Morrissey appreciates about his improvising actors: they produce perfect – unpredictable, illogical, but somehow just right – details that normal scripting would be too bound by formula or plausibility to produce. Similarly, Holly assures her young customer that she won't use a needle even as she wields one: "It's not a needle," she says. "It's like a penicillin shot.... You don't trust me?" These are Morrissey's favorite moments. "Nobody would have written that stuff," he says. "These are the reversals you would never write. And the way she says it is absolutely brilliant."

(Incidentally, guess who won the Best Supporting Actress Oscar for 1970. Nope, Helen Hayes did, for *Airport*. Holly Woodlawn was not even nominated, though Karen Black for *Five Easy Pieces* and Sally Kellerman for *M*A*S*H* were.)

As Joe lacks the dignity and self-respect that impress us in Holly, he remains the passive narcissist that Dallesandro portrayed in *Flesh*. The later film's picaresque plot line centers on his humiliation and impotence, as his hard drugs have rendered him incapable of an erection. In this respect, *Trash* can be read as a rebuttal to *Flesh,* for it moves from Joe's professional potency to his junked impotence. It further deglamorizes the "liberated" society. The second film opens with a close-up of Joe's pimpled bum, while Geri (Geri Miller) futilely tries to fellate him into an erection. "You used to be dynamite, Joe. Don't you remember? Don't you miss it?" she asks. Geri's sensitivity, sense, and her generous attempts to arouse him recall the actress's warmth and pathos in their *Flesh* scene. The siliconed breasts that she had discussed getting she now disports as she again dances for the still-oblivious Joe, to the song "Mama, Look at Me Now." Joe receives less sensitive treatment by the upscale women who address his impotence later.

The characters' continuity across the two films at once reminds us of the artifice of filmmaking, yet makes the characters seem paradoxically real. This is especially true for the gloriously persuasive femininity allowed the transvestite actor, Holly Woodlawn. It begins with her first dress, which literally labels her as a woman: a shift emblazoned with one "ideal" woman's measurements (36"–22"–?). But Holly's womanhood becomes wholly accepted. As John Russell Taylor put it, "What we get is what nearly all cinema ultimately is, the physical embodiment of private dreams. And it works here so immaculately because the people are so scrupulously respected in their quite possibly crazy integrity."[26] As we believe Holly's conception

43

of herself as a woman, we accept her conviction that Joe, like the rest of her trash, can and should be salvaged.

In the film's most moving scene, when Holly is unable to arouse Joe, she reverts to masturbating on a beer bottle (a Miller's High Life, as it happens). As she climaxes, she reaches down to grip Joe's hand. Joe's eyes water into tears as she begs him to kick his drug habit so she can have him instead of the beer bottle. Morrissey draws a compelling romantic moment out of most unpromising materials.

Furthermore, the beer-bottle masturbation dramatizes Morrissey's acceptance of his transvestite performer as a woman. Perhaps unique in American cinema, this scene validates our most neglected sexual minority, the transsexual. Morrissey accepts the biological being that his performer aspires to be. This contrasts the transvestite appearance of Jackie Curtis and Candy Darling in *Flesh,* that is, wearing a different gender instead of becoming one. In a film culture that exclusively accepts heterosexual norms, and that plays gender changes only for laughs (as in *Some Like It Hot* and *Tootsie*), with the comforting impulse of a plot necessity (evading gangsters or getting a job, respectively), Morrissey alone accepted a performer's assumption of a different gender.[27] Of course, there is a huge difference between the transvestite and the transsexual. But in presenting the transvestite Holly Woodlawn as the complete woman, Holly, Morrissey accepts the biological transformation of a gender as an honest, psychological imperative, to a degree no other American film has done yet.

As Joe lies on his mattress below Holly's bed, the geography of the sleeping arrangements assumes a metaphorical weight. It's not just that Holly lives on a level above Joe's. She has a capacity to salvage – if not resurrect – the junked (whether the garbage she finds or the man she loves). It's a capacity he lacks, especially as he continues to resist her. Moreover, the bed that ought to unite the lovers now separates them, as Joe fails to dedicate his remnant sexual energy to his lover. As the bed bisects the frame it traps both characters in their respective boxes, across which only Holly's grasp can reach. At the same time, the centering of the bed in the frame gives the domestic scenes a formal elegance surprising even in Morrissey's aesthetic. Typically, it is an elegance that emerges from the subject, that seems discovered on-site, not imposed in the interests of glossing the subject over with style.

More obviously than *Flesh, Trash* is a black comedy. The yuppie Jane tells of a Grosse Pointe High School junkie friend (oddly, named Danny Davito) who was run over by a tank during the Detroit riots. When Bruce asks, "Was he drugged?" she replies with the clear logic of the idiot: "Well, he must have been. Who would miss a tank?" The more sympathetic Geri's attempts to arouse Joe include (ludicrously) appealing to his mind by talking politics: "Do you think we should have war?" Yet despite the absurdity of the conversation and the grotesqueness of the characters, Morrissey is still playing variations on his basic form, situation comedy. His characters are locked into demented parodies of family life, especially Holly and her sister (who seduces Joe by saying the two sisters used to "make it"). More to the point, the supposedly straight world – as represented by the newlyweds and by the social worker – is kinkier because it is less feeling than that of the social underlings. Overall, Morrissey's target is the illusion of freedom and fulfillment that obtains in a world where (as the sister tells Joe) "You really shouldn't worry. Nowadays anything goes."

But there are limits, the mortal flesh and waning spirit sped by self-abuse. Even then, we reject the social worker's conclusion: "You're garbage! Low-life!" For Morrissey's characters have spoken for themselves beyond his moral critique and we have been touched. As John Russell Taylor pointed out, "Behind practically everything that happens and is said there is a quiet, almost suppressed anguish over the evanescence of experience, the search for something that lasts, and the retreat, most evidently in Joe's case, into drugs as a deadener."[28] There truly is a moving evanescence in the film's ending. Holly, in her futile but indomitable devotion to her discarded man, offers, "Joe, lemme suck your cock." But the lovers remain immobile on opposite edges of the frame.

Absurdly in this economic context, Joe has a pet, a huge hound named Caesar. The dog's unpredictable glances and behavior enhance the film's feel of unplanned, oh-too-sadly-real life. Recalling the restless lap cat in Warhol's *Harlot* (1964), it also provides a domestic bridge like the baby in *Flesh*, a surrogate for the child Holly would like to have. The dog also points to the poor couple's desire for middle-class respectability. With her woman's instinct for survival, it is Holly, not Joe, who applies for the welfare that will give her respectability. In the opening scene of *Flesh*, the couple's sexual freedom is "undercut by an acceptance of the conventional division of roles in bourgeois marriage."[29] In *Trash*, the deprived couple craves the stability of a normal life. In contrast, the architect and his wife enjoy economic freedom, education, and class, which have "liberated" them from traditional values and left them hollow to the core. To Morrissey, "the old-fashioned middle-class values are so much more interesting than the freedom." And he had to cast a female impersonator to play the plucky heroine because "Girls are just blasé, they're just like boys today."[30]

Perhaps the marquee lights that announce the film point to the romantic

45

ideal that Bruce and Jane imagine they are living, an image of American life that *Trash* entirely denies. When Bruce tells Jane to watch Joe shoot up, she glamorizes her ambivalent squeamishness: "I don't want to look... I'm not interested... I just want to have fun, a gay time." But she looks at Joe with the exploitative security of both the affluent woman and the voyeur from the time she catches him at burglary. Her "gay time" is the life of style and titillation, heedless of the social and moral reality of the world. In sum, Jane is the typical commercial film viewer whose sensibility *Trash* is calculated to upset. For Kinder and Houston, the bottle-masturbation scene "attacks with poignant satire the American myth of total love in spotless surroundings, of clean togetherness in cineramic omnipotence. Instead, *Trash* urges us to accept as valuable the limited, the tawdry, the vulnerable, and the sordid because they are the common qualities of the human condition."[31]

Technically, *Trash* represents a major advance for Morrissey. Individual shots are more carefully conceived, as we saw in the bedroom geography. The documentary inserts of street life, which root the narrative in the real world, are more carefully pointed to the characters' involvement. Morrissey's static tripod camera suggests a cool, detached eye. He depends solely upon the zoom to move in on or away from the characters in the room. Even then, Morrissey was criticized because (as Greg Ford put it) "his style misses the virtual autism of some of Warhol's finest images, their near-complete lack of stylistic effect. But fortunately, few of Morrissey's cuts have any real emotional connotation.... *Trash*'s forced primitivity, its calculated rawness, its deliberate anti-artiness frees numerous fragments of crude reality, vivid, memorable."[32] Without selling out, Morrissey drew closer to the conventional narrative (not necessarily commercial) devices, where establishing shots set up shrewdly chosen pans or cut-in close-ups.

Morrissey wanted to elaborate on Holly's desire for domestic normalcy in a sequel he planned in 1979 but could not realize. In *Trash II*, the family was to have gotten the money to move out of their slum when a cab hit one of their kids. Holly was now a housewife, Joe was a cabbie shooting up in the Bronx, and their child was selling dope in school. The *Flesh* films would have segued neatly into Morrissey's street films.

Heat (1972)

After his political comedy *Women in Revolt* (see next chapter), Morrissey resumed the one-word focus of his trilogy. *Heat* opens with a statement of social/historical reflection: the symptomatic closing of the Fox studio on Sunset Boulevard in 1971. By implication, the loss of this old order set the characters adrift in the poststudio world. As Morrissey misses the lost rigor of the Jesuits, the old studio here functions as a lost social order, as the Mafia will in *Spike of Bensonhurst*. The eponymous heat includes the lotusland climate, the amoral torpor that lets anything go, and the feverish lusts for sensuality, fortune, and fame.

The opening statement also sets off the common assumption that the film is a reworking (but not a remake)[33] of *Sunset Boulevard*. A sleazy studio producer (Lester Persky) celebrates his former wife/actress as a package: "Even in those days, people knew bodies." That's a pragmatic version of Gloria Swanson's "we had faces then." Morrissey knows that the Hollywood flesh factory fantasizes bodies more than faces. In Morrissey's twist, the Gloria Swanson figure of an aged star desiring a comeback is replaced by Joe Dallesandro as an over-the-hill child actor. Even this young man's appearance is considered obsolete in television: the agent is now looking for "a young Elliot Hoffman type." Morrissey says he "thought of *Heat* originally as *The Blue Angel*, with Sylvia Miles as the sensitive person who humiliates herself for this traveling entertainer who's amoral."[34]

The mythic world of glamour and romance Morrissey counters with the theme of consumption. His film is about the Hollywood types' eternal quest for a meal ticket. *Heat* studies a community of derelicts around the Tropicana Motel pool. The central character is Joey Davis (Joe Dallesandro), a former child star on a Western TV series, *The Big Ranch* (translation: an unzipped Johnny Crawford of *The Rifleman*), who is now trying to establish himself as a rock and roll singer. He pays his rent by having sex with the grotesque landlady, Lydia (Pat Ast, who in David Bailey's documentary film on Warhol recalls being a classmate of Barbra Streisand). Lydia insists that "This L.A. is going to the dogs, but not here, not in this place." But her world of lazy license in no way evokes a lost, better time. For Morrissey, "Every society, no matter how degenerate, demands some kind of standards. I find this very comical, but also very human."

Joey then lives off of an affair with Sally Todd (Sylvia Miles). When he makes love to her on the shadowed staircase of her mansion, the image is of her downward and his upward mobility – and the mutual exploitation that Morrissey sees everywhere as free sex. Joey also lets himself be sexually tapped by Sally's daughter, Jessie, who has a baby (played by the Dallesandros' real-life baby) and is involved in a relationship with a sadistic lesbian. He is also taken by Harold (Harold Childe), the lover of Sally's ex-husband Sidney, and himself a former child star. In short, Joey is a male version of the passive, exploited starlet who casting-couched herself to delusions of Hollywood promise.

As he melts into the immoral torpor, Joey's lovemaking is passive, often offhanded. He reaches back and up, without looking or feeling, to fondle his landlady's breasts after consenting to receive her massage. In one telling composition, as Joey sits absentmindedly on a couch, Jessie (Andrea Feldman) writhes ecstatically with his booted foot in her crotch. Joey is most passive when rejecting Jessie's advances. Even as he says no, he lets her proceed.

Morrissey shifts the emotional weight from Dallesandro to Miles. When Morrissey's camera caressingly pans along Dallesandro's body or holds on a profile close-up, it typifies all of the characters' self-absorption. Hence this postcoital pillow talk, which interrupts a tongue-kiss:

SALLY: Did you think I was a good actress, Joey?
JOEY: Mmm hmm. Let's see if I can get some work. Do you think you'll be able to get me some work?

That the film may be intended as a mood piece about male alienation may be inferred from the precredit shot of Dallesandro lingering on the abandoned sound stage. But Morrissey allows fuller pathos to the aged actress. Although she is shrill and ludicrous in her conversations, especially those with her daughter, to Sidney she admits a genuine need and affection for her young lover. Coming in the middle of a quarrel over money, this brief glimpse into a heart is all the more touching. It suggests she could be more than "a walking checkbook" to her daughter and lover, though that was at least partially her view of her husbands.

In addition to Sally, there are two other parody mothers. At the motel the presiding harridan caricatures maternal authority. But even Lydia has a delicacy, of which we are granted a glimpse. She may seem absurdly self-deluding when she preens with a fan, tugs at her too-shorts or dissolves into foldout poses. But she shows a sad romantic dying to emerge when she calls Joey's fondling of her nipple "just like a little bit of semi-heaven," a sentiment all the more touching for its reserved qualifiers ("a little bit," "semi") and Joe's lack of interest. So too, her sincerity and surprising self-awareness when she explains why she always reads love comics: "Well, if you can't get it all the time you have to make a joke of it." In the same vein, she asks Gary, "What have you lived, to know what beauty is?" As John Weightman rightly observed at the film's release, "Either Warhol or Morrissey has an extraordinarily keen sense of the pathetic fragility of

Joey's patrons: Lydia (Pat Ast) and Sally (Sylvia Miles) in *Heat*.

beauty and the aggressive beauty of ugliness."[35] By now we know that touch was Morrissey's.

The third "mother" is Sally's daughter. Jessie is caught in two bleak parental relationships, one as daughter and one as parent. She openly admits caring only for her mother's money. She's drawn away from her lesbian relationship not so much by Joey's sexual appeal as by her desire to come between him and her mother. Hence the ambivalence when Jessie first tells Joey about her: "She's great. She's my mother. We don't get along too well." The middle sentence explains the difference between the other two. So too, her glee when Sally finds Joe being fellated by Harold. An obvious loose fish herself, Jessie describes her mother in terms unsentimental even for Hollywood: "She was a cheap chorus girl." In an inspired non sequitur Andrea Feldman adds, "Whore all over town. She got into L.A., says 'Katch-kelle, Bubbelle, can I have a cup of coffee?' " The Yiddish (for "little goose" and "darling") is the kind of unscriptable notion that suggests a real mind at free association.

Jessie threatens to feed her son "antibiotic baby food," has no under-standing of his crying, and sedates him so she can go out with Sally and

Joey. She even carries him in a shopping bag, "packaging" or commodifying yet another helpless modern creature. As Marsha Kinder and Beverle Houston read the adult-baby theme: "In the trashy world of *Heat,* everyone wants to star in his own movie, and that means playing the role of baby who is desired, pampered and cared for." The only real baby in the film is "rejected by all the 'adults,' who are trying to satisfy their own infantile needs."[36] The adults are all unmatured child stars.

Yet Jessie (especially as embodied by Andrea Feldman) provides some of the film's most engaging spirit. However wacky, she at least has a saving zest. She gives the film its most intense statement of survival: "I like all the health foods. You name it, I'll eat it!" Though that follows upon an unappetizing litany of her latest fad (a diet of olive oil, salt and pepper, artichokes, avocadoes, and nuts), it places Jessie on the side of the self-asserters, the eater instead of the eaten. That also applies to how and why she seduces Joey.

Within these skeletal family relationships the characters are absurd. Jessie introduces herself to Joey: "You probably don't remember me. I saw you on that TV show?" Jessie interrupts Joey's first sex with Lydia, screaming in pain as the swimming pool chlorine penetrates the cigarette burns received from lover Bonnie. Bonnie's threat to kill herself – when she learns Jessie took Joey to Sally's for lunch – keeps Jessie from getting a needed check. The film is full of interruptions because it's about fragile minds and brittle relationships.

Despite the vacant lives and babble, the characters touchingly demonstrate their needs. At the motel are two brothers who perform a nightclub act: "We do some singing and some dancing and then we have a little sex on stage.... It's a living." The younger (Eric Emerson) is a mute who walks around in a skirt, compulsively masturbating. Though his brother (Gary Koznocha) says they only have sex on stage, he's still jealous when Jessie starts to help the younger brother reach climax. This is a black comic view of fraternity.

Or as Sally – desperately trying to believe herself – puts it, "Every day holds some kind of hope for something great, right?" Sally advises Joey to "unlearn" how to be negative. She enters her doomed relationship with Joey urgently denying its inevitable outcome: "But you won't be mean to me, will you? Like all the rest of them?... Don't do this to me and then leave me, Joe." She even has a moral explanation for her many marriages: "I always marry every man I have an affair with." So she's all the more hurt when Joe insists upon leaving before breakfast, when she learns of his previous use by the landlady, and when she fears losing him to her daughter. After Jessie fellates Joey ("Does my mother do that as well as I do?"), Sally seems pathetically naive when she tells Jessie that Jessie can't go out with Joey and her: "You have to stay home to read tonight.... Have a hot cup of cocoa before you go to sleep." In this topsy-turvy world Joey can call Jessie "a sick lesbian" for being so openly attracted to him.

For actress Sally, her daughter is just playing a role. Her lesbianism is a "phase," a part played to spite her, as if no being exists beyond the artifice of a performance. "Don't tell me you're a lesbian, because I know it's a temporary thing," she tell her daughter. "I won't allow it.... I told you not to wear pants; why do you do that?" She handles Jessie's seduction of Joey by seeing life as a failed performance of a role: "She can't even make a good dyke," she says. Sally fears that exposure to Jessie's life-style will make her baby grandson a lesbian too.

At the end everyone has failed. Sidney's relationship with Harold turns out to be no more secure than Sally's relationships with either Joey or her daughter. The various child stars have matured into victims of their own freed sexuality. Sally even fails in her last melodramatic gesture, an attempt to shoot Joey. Morrissey's last shot holds on the shimmering motel pool. As the plot parallels situations in *Sunset Boulevard,* this closing shot artic- ulates the difference of his Hollywood morality play. Morrissey's heroes don't end with a bang, but with a whimper. There are no bullets in Sally's gun and never were: she was never a Swanson star but a B-grade never- was condemned to a fate worse than oblivion, television game shows and made-for-TV "features." So into the pool goes the empty gun instead of the disappointing gigolo. No body floats in this pool because everyone is in a deadening heat, like Eliot's hollow men, stuffed with the straw of pathetic solitude and lust in the name of freedom. There are no wise and witty voices from the afterlife, no memories of adventure, because everyone is locked into reflexes of selfish desire and ineluctable despair. Of this world Morrissey's unvarnished naturalism provides a more appropriate approach than Billy Wilder's (and Hollywood's) rhetoric.

Despite its sophistication, *Heat* nevertheless conveys Morrissey's crucial impression of a lived rather than a scripted life, even if his characters are given to theatrical self-projections. In fact, at a postpremiere New York Film Festival panel discussion, Elia Kazan rose from the audience to state how moving he found the film, especially the mystery around its characters' unexplained and unsimplified motivations. As in all three films, much of the power derives from our sense that we are watching characters living out what they are, even as they play roles. So even the pro, Sylvia Miles, seems to be living like a Factory persona when she interrupts intercourse to ask Joey "Do I look alright? I have an image to keep up."

Further, as Greg Ford shrewdly pointed out, the Hollywood context redefines the nonacting Dallesandro as "a bastard descendent of the classic passive Western hero," the strong silent type of American manhood, archetypically defined by The Virginian and Gary Cooper, but "with the modesty and abstention subtracted."[37] What seemed most aberrant in the Dallesandro features, a passive, inexpressive center, turns out to be Hollywood's mythic main line. Even the film's sexual license is articulated to mainstream Hollywood when Jessie expresses shock at the skin magazines in the porn stores and at Candace Bergen's implied masturbation of Art Garfunkle in Mike Nichols's Carnal Knowledge. Of course, she expresses this indignation while she helps Eric masturbate.

Dallesandro's continuing persona makes his Greenwich Village whore another version of the flesh market of Hollywood, even (or especially) when he's decked out in stylish new clothes. For all the bleaching light and wider El Lay spaces, it's still Morrissey's familiar world of soulless sloths and personae of prostituted personality. As Yvette Biro contends, throughout the trilogy "there pulsates the fatigue of the flesh, a collapse and disintegration remindful of garbage heaps, and an energy-consuming heat.... The style seems to be evaporating. The unattractive moments of vegetation take a comic turn, and irony is created by a finite transparency, as if in the wake of a deep-raking and indifferent X-ray beam."[38] Not all of the major critics were this sensitive to the film's effect. Pauline Kael dismissed it as "a slack, depressive Paul Morrissey version of Sunset Boulevard.... meant to be a funny exploitation movie, but the comic moments are rare."[38]

All three of these films may seem but to document their layabouts' empty lives with Warhol's "recorder" gaze. But implicit in all three is Morrissey's doubled emotional involvement. On the one hand he has the moralist's anger at the characters wasting their lives, spending themselves in drugs, prostitution, and betrayal of their loved ones. The films belie the glamour of sixties street life. The first two films include scenes in which young outsiders are introduced to the destruction they have sought (the hustlers in Flesh, young Johnny in Trash). As Sidney observes in Heat, "It's the way kids are today." On the other hand, Morrissey feels for his characters' pathetic needs and for their fleeting self-awareness. Stripped to garbage, Holly can't (to her credit) surrender her silly silver platform shoes even to get the respectability of welfare. Her Joe just weeps at his inability to go on methadone, which would help his lover off the long-necked beer bottle. In none of his incarnations can Joe decline someone's invitation to exploit him sexually, however the act may betray himself or his lovers. For Joe in all three films has the same lack of vision he speaks about to Holly's sister when she seduces him in *Trash:* He can't distinguish human will and restraint from animal reflex. That scene has a riveting grotesqueness that begins with Holly's sister's first invitation – "You ever make it with a pregnant woman?" – and continues with the unprecedented image of a large-bellied woman proceeding to mount her sister's lover even though he's an impotent junkie. This is a triumph of matter over mind.

All three films have a subtle structure that belies their anecdotal rambling. In all three there is a tension between the hero's domestic situation and his encounters with people outside. The terms "private" and "public" lives don't apply, because Morrissey's point is the dissolution of this distinction. In their license his characters make public business out of their private nature; the intimacy of Morrissey's filming in turn makes their private lives a public spectacle. The characters' helpless freedom and the cinema's brave new candor have made public property of the "privates." Unrestrained self-indulgence has erased the integrity of the self.

The films were not planned from the outset as a trilogy, yet they were developed into a unit. Morrissey moves from his hero's physical potency in *Flesh,* through impotence in *Trash,* to the renewed vigor but most active corruption in *Heat.* In all three, dependence upon the flesh betrays the waste of life. In shifting from the hovels of the East Village to the luxurious spaces of Los Angeles, Morrissey establishes a national and cultural range for his moral criticism. His subject is America's nationwide bohemia, the modishly liberated.

There is a similar reduction across the trilogy in the characters' primary objectives. In *Flesh* the characters crave adult versions of the purity we glimpse in Joe's scene with the baby. But that's impossible once the appetite outgrows the cupcake. In *Trash* the central need is self-respect. In *Heat* the need is for that Hollywood product, romance, a need earnestly felt by all the women but from which Joey's vain ambition disqualifies him except as a commodity. Here, romantic delusions can be as debilitating as dope.

The last film elaborates on a metaphor only flirted with in the first two films: the family. All three films abound with references to family. The traditional basic social unit is depicted solely in terms of betrayal and destruction. Sally's five husbands; the brothers' professional sex; and Jessie's tensions with her mother, her lesbian lover, her son, her father, and her mother's lover, all provide a virtual encyclopedia of family disruption, L.A. style. This is the nuclear family, exploded. *Heat* makes explicit and rounded a theme that lingers in all of Morrissey's films since the silent interlude in *Flesh*.

For the family is the quintessential social structure, the personal form of an institution from which one should be able to draw emotional, moral, even economic sustenance. Morrissey's use of family may provide what Joan Mellen found distinctive in "Warhol's" characters: "Part of the sweetness of his characters and the films derives from the sense of community in the midst of their adversity which they develop toward each other. They create an insulated world where hostile voices of moral judgment cannot label and degrade their relationships."[40] In *Flesh* the basic family center is violated when the wife sends her baby's father out to prostitute himself to buy her lover an abortion. Here Morrissey uses the family as an arena for his moral apocalypse. In *Trash* the layered sleeping arrangements and the wife's frustrations and rage indicate the range of ways that the hero's abuse has gone beyond his self. And *Heat* shows, through the family, how a loss of social order results in self-obsessed drifters.

Finally, the three films seem to grow toward an increasing sensitivity to women. Despite the films' focus on Dallesandro, their emotional center usually falls upon an eloquent, feeling woman: Geri Miller, Holly Woodlawn, or Sylvia Miles. In part this may be due to Morrissey's observation that women are more articulate and expressive than men: "The volatile parts go to women because you can't have a hysterical man – unless he's George C. Scott," Morrissey says. "Volatile females with passive men is the great story of today. It's great material for comedy. Men aren't dramatic unless they're beating someone up."[41] In part, Morrissey made this choice because of the especial flamboyance and ease in performance he found in his transvestites.[42] The virtue Dallesandro brought his roles was

> a brooding intensity which you see as a realistic effect.... You lose the spontaneity when you realize somebody's thinking the hell out of their part. That's why Joe is so good, because he never has the notion that he's supposed to dwell upon what he's doing. He just goes and does it and he does it very realistically, with a certain amount of strength. Strong characters are hard to come by."[43]

But in his women Morrissey discovers the truer strengths of sense and will.

3
Approaching Politics

Morrissey generally denies making political films: "I'm very political, but I don't think it belongs in film. All politics change with the wind, so it's silly to put politics in movies. The politics in my movies is like the sex. It's always, always there to be funny." But in the development of independent cinema, there has always been a "politics of the nonpolitical."[1] Simply to make an independent, noncommercial (or especially anticommercial) film is a political act. This is especially clear in someone with Morrissey's moral intensity and social concern. His resistance to commodification is as much a political stance as an aesthetic one. So, too, his disgust with the mass marketing not just of drugs and sex but of the religion of self-indulgence.

Ken Kelman defined American underground film as essentially the rebellion of imaginative and spiritual energies against the repressiveness of Hollywood (the macro fantasy industry, if you will) and American society. Morrissey's work would fall into Kelman's category of "outright social criticism and protest"[2] – but with one difference: Morrissey's target is libertinism, not repression. Or, more precisely: his target is the repression of restraint. In three films Morrissey extended the sexual comedy of his *Flesh* trilogy into a consistent political statement. They give his moral vision a societal dimension. *Women in Revolt* (1971) is an ambivalent comedy about women's liberation. *L'Amour* (1972) and *Madame Wang's* (1981) are companion pieces that vary the traditional plot of the innocent abroad. The reflective vagabonds in the latter two films express Morrissey's comic view of the women's liberation movement. But the films' most common denominator is Morrissey's cynical critique of American civilization (which in context seems to be an oxymoron, like "jumbo shrimp" or "common sense").

Three women revolt against their gender's various oppressions and join forces in a feminist movement, the PIGs – Politically Involved Girls.[3] The term may seem sexist but it parallels the unfortunate acronym for Status Of Women committees. Nor is the name as reductive as SCUM ("Society for Cutting Up Men"), the militant feminist organization claimed by Valerie Solanis, who shot Warhol. After Warhol's shooting, one might well expect an antifeminist reflex in the Warhol Factory at the time. "Andy and I used to say that we were the first feminist casualties," the also-wounded art critic/ curator Mario Amaya jokes.[4] But when the film was made, feminism had already grown from individual campaigners into a mass, even international, movement. This was ten years after President Kennedy established the Committee on the Status of Women, five years after Betty Friedan became founding president of the National Organization of Women, three after the first mass action of women at the Miss America pageant of 1968, and one year after Kate Millett's *Sexual Politics* was published.[5] In this light, much of Morrissey's comedy derives from his heroines' surprising vagueness about the movement. More typically, he draws pathos from their inability to reconcile the movement's intellectual objectives with their physical needs. As the film stars three histrionic transvestites – Candy Darling, Jackie Curtis, and Holly Woodlawn – its ambiguous viewpoint on the nature of women, their treatment and their response, runs deeper than the litter of PIG gags.[6] The film respects its women and sympathizes with their perception of systemic injustice, even though its political statement may be tempered by the broad comedy.

Both in their initial predicaments and in their fates, the three heroines project a spectrum of feminist sensibility. The leader, the most ardent and articulate feminist, is Jackie Curtis, who says, "We're tired of being exploited." The virgin Jackie seeks to transcend her colleagues' baser drives, saying, "Candy's after pussy, Holly's after cock. . . . What I'm after is something – intangible." She repeats that "only one percent of the women in the United States makes over ten thousand dollars a year." In her politics, Jackie keeps a houseboy, Dusty (Dusty Springs), to do her nails and clean her apartment. She sprays him with industrial strength deodorant and throws lit matches at him to speed his housework. Otherwise she banishes men from her flat, saying to a hapless fellow whom Holly has dragooned into carrying up a gift houseplant, "Take your balls and go." Jackie teaches Holly that women are more fun intellectually and spiritually. Or as she tells

Paul Morrissey directs Jackie Curtis in *Women in Revolt* while Andy Warhol operates the camera.

her houseboy, "Don't you know there's something more beautiful in this world than – that thing – between your legs? Haven't you heard of Women's Liberation?... Cunt is beautiful.... You know that males are inferior to females." When we see the houseboy's limp penis flopping about his housework, Morrissey endorses Jackie's undercutting of male authority. In one shot the framing holds on the drooping penis but cuts out the man's head and face. Reducing him from personality to penis, it fragments the male character into sexual parts, as our culture has traditionally objectified the image of woman (and as Morrissey did in his close-ups of Geri Miller's newly siliconed breasts in *Trash*).

But Jackie herself betrays the cause after buying sex with a Mr. America, Johnny Minute (Johnny Kemper). She initially regards him as a kindred "victim of the dude culture" because he, like women, is a sex object. But she hires him, to her own undoing. First he forces her to fellate him, which only confirms her sense of women's exploitation, even when it's the woman who buys the man. "Girls are supposed to like this?" She asks, "This is what's been going on all these years?" To emphasize her gagging ordeal, the camera holds for a long time on the stud's buttocks, clutched by Jackie's painted nails. But with more conventional sex he converts her from the cause:

JOHNNY: Are you gonna come?
JACKIE: I dunno. I think I'm gonna go.... I'm coming. Oh, now I know what we're against!

Abandoned by this man, Jackie proceeds to blow PIG money on a succession of men who advertise in the *East Village Other*. When we last see her, she is back in Bayonne, a single parent, talking on the phone to her mother. As a result of her heterosexual experiment she has receded into domestica. Her ostensible contentment crumbles when her baby starts to cry and she says, "I love that baby. It's like an angel. That's the best thing a woman can do. ... Ma, I was happy as a lesbian.... [*to the baby:*] Shut the fuck up.... Whaddyamean I'm not even-tempered?"

The other two heroines play variations on Jackie's destructive self-service. Candy Darling plays a bored "society deb socialite" ("I'm young. I have a right to live!"), who wistfully sings "Give me a man who does things, who does things to my heart." She lends the PIG movement her status and glamour in order to launch her own film career. A painfully prolonged seduction/rape by a seedy agent (Michael Sklar) sets her course. By letting her directors "fuck the daylights out of her," she becomes a no-talent star of Italian exploitation films, Jules Verne adaptations, and *The Fornicon*. In the last scene a lesbian journalist (played by a man, Jonathan Kramer) from *The New York Times* strips away Candy's pretensions and confronts her sordid past. There are rumors of incest with her brother and that Candy missed the funeral of her parents, who in shame committed suicide. The reporter seeks even more lurid confessions: "The people want filth." After assaulting the star and tearing her white paper backdrop, the journalist leaves Candy shattered on the floor: "I think I got the story I came for." When the thin photographer tries to help Candy up, he collapses under her nonmythic weight.

Holly initially revolts against being dependent upon a man. In her first scene she fights off her possessive lover, Marty (Marty Kove):

MARTY: You're mine!
HOLLY: Never, never. Bastard!

But he beats and rapes her. As his limp penis is visible – and stays limp – throughout the rape, the image suggests that his violence toward women is a matter of a larger impotence. Holly fondles a knife threateningly as she resolves finally to leave him. But the women's violence goes no further than administering a simulated (through the jeans) enema – a symbolic rape reversal – to a hardhat streetworker who has insulted two feminist pickets. Despite her declarations of independence, Holly cannot resist temptation. In several scenes, while Jackie lectures feminism, Holly in the foreground molests some convenient man. At film's end she is a vagrant Bowery wino. All three liberated women remain trapped in their social/biological roles.

Or do they? The three main socially/biologically trapped women are played by transvestites, that is, by social/biological men whose will and imagination have enabled them to "become" women. In one three-in-a-bed scene, while Jackie lectures on the significance of a woman, Betsy Ross, making the American flag, Holly flirts with anal oral sex on manservant Dusty. For no apparent reason, he wears a bra as he lies between the women. Morrissey recalls that the bra just happened as a spontaneous gag, adding to the confusion of gender roles. But poetically it balances the flag and bra as symbols of political control. (Both were subjects of protest burning at the time.) Further, it displaces the surprise of seeing Holly's utterly male chest. Here a physical gag makes for metaphysical spins.

As Greg Ford remarked, this "stupefyingly complex" film is "much more than a campy joke on Women's Liberation or on moviedom's most maudlin mellers. Many pressures and abrasions between discordant realities are in-carnated by Candy Darling, many different vying selves convexly micro-scoped on her face: stamped on, most superficially, is the iconic, synthetic and manufactured Hollywood blonde, but with the layer of glistening glitter, is a real woman, and, underlying this, a real man."[7] There's an almost masculine resonance in her normally very feminine voice when Candy orders her comrades: "Would you all sit down and act like ladies?"

This is anti-illusionist cinema. As Parker Tyler contends, we are not sup-posed to accept the characters portrayed by transvestite performers com-pletely as women. "Here the gimmick and the grandeur are all together. We never forget, nor are we meant to forget, that these 'actresses' are males. And they are most male when most absurdly pretending to be female." This mystery gives the film its "devious . . . pithy paradox" and "a rather awesome majesty," because its effect far exceeds its paraphrasable content.[8]

Typically, Morrissey filters his social concern through the media industry. Candy's ambition to become a Hollywood star while there is still a Hol-lywood to star in is a surrogate yearning for a classical moral order (as in *Heat* later). She yearns for a traditional attachment, however bathetic. The casting couch rape, the women's orchestration of financial patronage, the tussle over picketing, and the closing interview establish the theatrical element in social action and (in return) make the media the arena for political activity. The alternative is the political victimization of the apathetic. Further, as David James suggests, "The desire of biological males to become females is reproduced as the desire of women to become stars."[9] To Parker Tyler, the violence that concludes the interview and the film "provides a transcendent insight, piercing, and not without blood, into what the Marilyn Monroes and Jean Harlows of film history always used to be about.... Ours is a man's world; maybe it is a world ruled by male chauvinism."[10]

Though the film's primary piquancy lies in this psychic no-person's-land of genders, much of the film's improvisational wit is verbal. For example, Jackie is naively confident that nobody would ever suspect a schoolteacher and a high fashion model (Jackie and Holly respectively) of being lesbians if they lived together! "What do I need a plant for?" Jackie asks Holly. "I already have a shrub." Then there's Candy outsnobbing even Jane Forth: "Yes, I think everyone should live on Park Avenue. I agree with you, and since I live on Park Avenue and you live wherever you live, why don't you just stay home today?" Or Jackie's attempt to coax Candy into the movement:

JACKIE: Come down off the trapeze and into the sawdust.
CANDY: That's circus talk.

When the agent calls Candy a nobody, the couch-cast starlet insists "I'm everybody." She proceeds to express her (multiple) self by doing (not very good) imitations of Joan Bennett, Lana Turner, and Kim Novak as Jeanne Eagels, the latter a mythic vamp/victim squared.[11]

The film strikes an unsettling tension between its comedy and its feminism. Candy's seduction by the agent veers wildly between comedy and pathos. As Stuart Byron remarked of this "truly anguishing" spectacle, "No one can switch from comedy to tragedy with such effortless ease" as Morrissey.[12] To persuade a patroness that the women's liberation issue is more than just "an abstraction," Jackie makes a speech equating intercourse with rape — while Holly molests a man in a wheelchair. One woman reports being raped by her father when she was two years old. Another says she was raped by Hell's Angels when she was unconscious from drugs; she can no longer ride the subway because old men jerk off at her and follow her home. Yet amid these shocks — and at Jackie's behest! — a blonde strips to prove woman's superiority. The shocking confessions turn comical. When one woman remarks that policemen masturbate on their sticks, another recalls a cop who insinuated himself into her apartment in order to suck her toes and — "I can't tell any more."

This shock makes it difficult to accept David Bourdon's assumption that the film "was calculated to antagonize the women's liberation movement (and perhaps the gay liberation movement as well)."[3] It's also hard to accept Pauline Kael's dismissal: "The subject is really the fantasies of Andy Warhol's 'superstars'; the dialogue is flat and the camera seems glued to the blemishes on the performers' rumps and thighs."[4] It should not require critical hindsight to find the latter evidence not a failure of technique but a deliberate denial of Hollywood illusionism. To this debate Verina Glaessner provides a useful conclusion in her *Time Out* review: "Some find the film anti-women in its parody of the notion of a women's movement ... but after all, who better equipped to depict these male fantasies about women than transvestites?"[5]

In the interview with Candy Darling, the belligerent journalist calls "Women's Liberation ... so dated now, like the hula hoop." On balance Morrissey seems to have taken the issue as a social topic – capable of double-edged satire – rather than as a political cause. His point is not that the movement is either good or bad, wise or silly, but that like any political stance it is vulnerable to self-indulgence and folly. Especially when a cause is espoused by the media, it becomes just another incitement to license or to sell another commodity. His subject is not women's rights but the irrelevance of political movements to the individual life. The heroines are not saved by the cause they variously espouse. Instead they are defeated when they succumb to "liberation." However willing their rhetoric, their flesh proves weak. Even the most ardent "believers" in the movement succumb. To Morrissey, then, survival and human progress depend upon the individual's control of appetite and will, rather than on any political movement; his film about gender politics coheres with his other critiques of destructive liberty.

L'Amour (1972)

As the journalist in *Women in Revolt* thought women's liberation was as "dated" as the hula hoop, in *L'Amour* Morrissey optimistically assumed that the hippie life-style was already obsolete – a premature assumption at best. Two American college girls (Jane Forth and Donna Jordan), headbands rampant, join a married girlfriend (Patti d'Arbanville) in Paris to learn cosmopolitan culture. The film plays against the tradition of such Hollywood romances as George Cukor's *Girls About Town* (1931). In the City of Love these two innocents abroad only confirm their own personal and cultural limitations.

The film provides almost as dramatic an admixture of tones as *Women in Revolt*. Most of the film is romantic farce. Patti arranges for her schoolgirl friends to be transformed into Parisian beauties, shucking the silliness of the hippie image ("I don't know where you've been but you've got to do something about yourself"). But the farce has an edge. Again the "liberation" is suspect. The hippies become gold diggers. As Morrissey prophetically told William Wolf, "It is logical that what has to follow the hippie generation will be a generation with interest in money and material things. ... Today, kids at 12 or 14 think the Establishment is the people who walk around with long hair and take drugs."[6] And so it came to pass that the beatnik begat the hippie and the hippie begat the yuppie. In a society that has lost its moral bearings, the only codes of conduct are fluctuating fads and fashion.

The film's glossy romanticism is subverted by bathroom satire with the entrance of the girls' suitors. Donna's Michael (Michael Sklar) is an American, heir to a deodorant block fortune derived from perfuming the pissoirs of Paree. That is to say, the status of the affluent American is based on the toilet, Morrissey's icon of contemporary culture. "The toilet metaphor logically applies to people who are refuse, living more in streets, alleys, gutters, and abandoned buildings than inside the traditional family," Morrissey says. It also suggests that the characters' values are merely cosmetic. So is Michael's desire to establish a family, having chafed under the pressures of his own. The human flotsam and jet-set jetsam crave the bourgeois respectability of the family. Jane's Max (Max Delys) is Michael's roommate, and wants Michael to adopt him. There are hints that Michael is Max's lover, but as there is no sex in the film this relationship is not certain. Michael says he met Max in a pissoir. Ever eking out respectability, the Puritan purist Max indignantly corrects him: "Not *in* a pissoir, *around* a pissoir."

Michael launches Donna's career as a high-fashion model by photographing her as she installs the deodorant cakes in the pissoirs. These shots are intended for the company's ads in *Vogue;* they equate the deodorant and the woman as commodities for media consumption, both perhaps destined to be flushed away. Though Michael marries Donna (primarily to improve his own image for his family and to facilitate the adoption), he prefers to keep eating (food) when he is in bed with her. As Greg Ford observes, the film's "anal-oral physical frailties ... blaspheme the feigned generic framework with its cutesy-touristic postcard plates of the Eiffel Tower and l'Arc de Triomphe."[7]

As usual, Morrissey changed the film's course in response to his cast. Originally intending the film to be a vehicle for Patti d'Arbanville and Jane

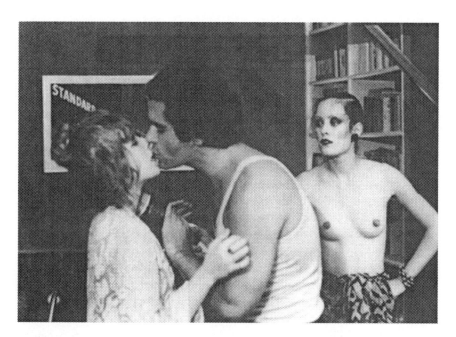

Jane Forth watches Max Delys court Donna Jordan in *L'Amour*.

Forth, Morrissey found their work not as interesting as Michael Sklar's (and d'Arbanville went away in midfilming). As a result, the film switches from the farce of American Airheads in Paris to the touching denouement that centers upon Michael's paradoxical character.

On the one hand, Michael is a miserly, bitter, selfish, vulgar clown, whose dumb jokes (punctuated with "Get it?") continually tax his lover's, his fiancée's, and the audience's patience. Even when offered a friendly discount on Karl Lagerfeld's designer dresses, Michael haggles over the price, as if determined to be loathsome. At his engagement party he invites "Everybody to the bar. Drinks on everybody!" As if to gloss over the banal basis of his family fortune, he composes ludicrous songs for a musical stage show – another cultural misfit saga, about a Cuban girl in a small American high school – in which he plans to cast his friends. As Michael sings and cavorts unengagingly, his romantic illusionism parallels his delusions about the stability of his affair with Max. This despite Max's steady insults ("If you need a lot of friends you have to pay for them.... If you want to touch my face you have to pay me.... You're too ugly"). Michael actually spits on Max because his wealth gives him that license. When Max asks Michael to adopt him ("I need a father"), Max is high up in a tree and Michael is gardening below, calling the plants his children. The Eden parody suggests the men have a vegetable relationship, lacking emotion and development.

But the worm turns . . . sympathetic. The film proves Morrissey's principle of trying to sympathize with all his characters. He finds a lyricism even in his characters' silliness, as is reflected in their scenes of play, especially when they roller-skate at the Palais de Chaillot. The intolerable Michael is allowed a genuine caring for his young roommate (and presumably lover) and a flash of self-knowledge: "The older I get, Karl, the more scared I get. There's something horrible about growing old alone." The scene recalls the older man's helpless dependence upon the narcissistic youth in *My Hustler* (1965). After overhearing Max confess that he does not really care for him, Michael releases Max, promising friendship or shelter as needed.

The last scene is a wordless montage concluding all of the central relationships. Michael touchingly watches Max walk away with Patti's husband Karl. Jane promises Max that she will remember him whenever she returns to Paris. That is, the romantic clichés of nostalgia are easier to handle than the responsibilities of a real relationship. She returns to her vapid life in America, calm of mind, no passion spent – or earned. In the last shot of the film, Michael and Donna are lost in the traffic of the city, an irregular couple (like everyone else) submerged into the anonymity of a long shot on the most romantic city in the world.

The film's central theme is the American's shallow worldliness. Patti is utterly cynical: "They're not even born a virgin in Paris." In contrast, the naive Donna relishes the hamburgers at La Coupole, which remind her of Horn and Hardart, the American automat chain. Michael matches her clinging to American ways: For dessert he produces Hershey bars and a Sara Lee. You can take the airhead out of America but you can't take America out of the airhead, not even in the seat of European culture. The characters' most acid lines cite America's garbage culture. Michael says Jane has "the brains of a used grapefruit rind." The smell of one pissoir reminds Jane of "a perfume my first boyfriend gave me." Admitting that she is more aroused by makeup than by men, Jane fends off Max's foreplay with her concern over her lipstick and hair. Her yearnings for American television with its talk shows, Mickey Mouse Club, and old movies, leave her quite impervious to Parisian culture (and to more: "Don't come in me. You can come but don't come in me."). Later she deflects his ardor with pleas of a chest rash, asthma, and diarrhea, all – like the American "culture" – debilitating afflictions. Morrissey's target is not just American culture, but the international with-it scene. So the Parisian persists in his ardor as ludicrously as the airhead deflects it.

The film marked a new commercial ambition for Morrissey and Warhol, hence its glossier look and the original song, sung by Mama Cass Elliot and composed by Sklar with Ben Weisman. The film had the factory's largest budget, almost $100,000, most of it spent on getting the cast to Paris. Its commercial ambition is clearest in its shift from male nudity to the more conventional exhibition of undressed women. But its commercialism did not modify Morrissey's acerbic view of the shallowness of American romanticism and culture.

Madame Wang's (1981)

Morrissey made his political perspective on American values more explicit in his second "innocent abroad" film, *Madame Wang's*. As the film begins and ends with the hero's view of the water, Morrissey seems for once to use a character to present his point of view. With his dark hair, height, and strong jaw, the character even looks like the young Paul Morrissey. Morrissey was unaware of this nuance at the time, though he refers to the character as a kind of alter ego. Typical of his self-effacement, however, Morrissey titled the film after his emblem of the corrupt culture rather than after his own identity figure. Oddly (of course), his hero/spokesman is Lutz (Patrick Schoene), an East German undercover KGB agent. He lands in Long Beach harbor to prepare for a communist invasion by connecting with America's leftist traitors, "the hippies, Americans who hate their country." His most compelling assignment: "Do you know where I can meet this Jane Fonda?" At her workout parlor he is instead confronted by the manager, a bulky crippled transvestite on a walker who nonetheless invites him to her ballet class!

Before that, the hero falls in with a hooker (Christina Indri, one of Morrissey's several beautiful nieces), who introduces him to yet another grotesque social subculture of human derelicts, living off the sale of scavenged trash. Her hysterical pimp Billy (Billy Edgar, from the Theatre of the Ridiculous) sniffs doorknobs and steals not only hubcaps but – what else? – toilet bowls (under the cops' noses), perverse emblems of American plenty. Billy introduces himself to Lutz while Lutz is using the toilet, Morrissey's emblem for the corrupt culture.

Billy welcomes the imminent communist invasion. "That's wonderful," he says. "It's about time somebody did something here." The characters' hunt for trash recalls Morrissey's second feature, but here it is a miniature of American capitalism, into which the communist is unfeelingly drawn ("You know what? It doesn't make any sense to me."). The whore's father

(Jimmy Maddows) – another transvestite and former hippie – dispatches Lutz to steal a rich man's car for him, because "It's not easy being a single parent, both mother and father, to two kids." The line is especially apt for a transvestite. He fattens his unspeaking but flatulent son Jason on Big Macs. He prefers that his daughter become a whore rather than suffer the "abuse" found in rock and roll; he's heard that they "take young girls on stage and urinate all over them." (Again, Morrissey assails the toilet liberal.) He put her on the streets "so she'd meet a better class of people." Vainly self-unaware, the fat father insists that his svelte, beautiful daughter "is the spittin' image of me." Not blessed with her father's delusions of worth, the whore works the streets at the swap meet, providing human merchandise. In the same spirit, we see waist-down mannequins in nylon pantyhose in the store window in front of which the whore picks up her second client. In contrast, a bearded behemoth recalls giving up his nylons and lipstick on his mother's advice in order to help mankind: "I was being redundant. ... My art was slipping away from me." Now he feels repaid through his spirituality. This hippie sermon is delivered while the characters sit on a pile of urinals, drinking tea.

Helping the whore teaches Lutz the low state of American innocence. First she is robbed by two young boys driving a Mercedes. One has his mother's permission to buy his sexual initiation. Then Lutz interrupts a customer's fantasy of playing diapered infant with the whore. In Morrissey's America there is no innocence even in childhood; there is only a perverse play at being innocent. The scene also equates sex with infantile toilet training. Compared to this American license, the East German subversive becomes a moral ideal. "If I have any success here it's because I have discipline," he says. For self-discipline he sometimes practices self-punishment by cutting his leg. He introduces the whore to the idea of telling the truth and even rejects her casual offer of sex. (Her vague "I just thought," of course, means that she didn't think.)

The film deploys two iconic settings. One is the empty Greek temple structure (the Long Beach Masonic Temple) in which the derelict characters squat. The building, with its Doric columns and classic lines incongruously set off against the California wasteland, was owned by Jack Simmons, who funded the film on the condition that it would be shot there. The building established Morrissey's basic metaphor: America as the dregs, the end of the glorious civilization that began in classical Greece. The false front on the building represents the sordid society's pretense to the ideals of Greek culture and democracy. It parallels Morrissey's use of mythic Paris in

66

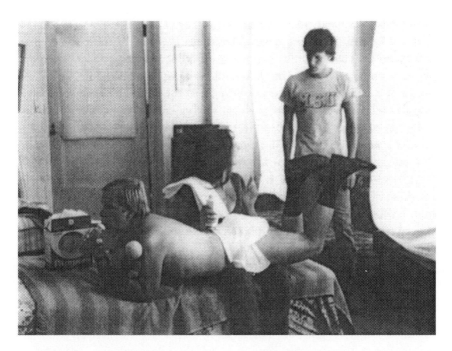

Lutz (Patrick Schoene) discovers his hooker friend (Christina Indri) pampering an infantile client in *Madame Wang's*.

L'Amour to score the American cultural shallows. In both cases the American culture pretends to a more hallowed tradition.

The second key setting is Madame Wang's, Los Angeles's most famous punk rock Chinese restaurant, subject of three articles in *Slash* and the cover of *Wet* magazine. That is to say, it is the symptomatic apogee of American culture, the current mythology that fits more truthfully than the classical mask of the Masonic tenement. The club represents America's faddish nihilism: As one character exults, "It's a lot of fun. Everybody's against everything." We're treated to performances by Phranque, "Madame Wang's most popular lesbian folksinger," who mumbles a tuneless love song to her junkie girlfriend, Charlotte:

> I like Charlotte,
> I think she's so swell,
> And if you don't like her
> Buster you can burn in Hell.

Other groups appear, such as The Butch, Boneheads, Mentors, and Leroy and the Lifters, who sing a new American anthem, "I need some good satisfaction." The ludicrous songs include "Oil My Body" and "Dream a While Scream a While." One habitué's costume, the Saturday Night Live image of a bee, extends Madame Wang's to the liberal iconoclasm of that popular television show. To perform in this club is the most passionate ambition of everyone the hero meets in the subculture. Despite their most earnest rehearsals, however, his transvestite friends are dismissed as having "no integrity – they're not ready for Madame Wang's."

But the communist Lutz is. At first he would "rather do anything – anything – than" perform at Madame Wang's. So he joins the scavengers and, having lost his phony papers, begins to grow American. He develops a need for a Mercedes, for numbered sports jerseys (that emblem of commercialized uniformity), and for individualism as star ego. Having failed as a pimp, he sinks to the lowest state of human degradation: the American punk rock hippie. He auditions at Madame Wang's. At first he seems entranced by the primitive rock music. But he hates its brutishness so much that he slashes himself with his switchblade rather than perform the spastic abandon Leroy taught him. His slashing seems to be American punk nihilism. But it is, rather, his communist self-discipline reviving his hatred of the music. He cuts his chest rather than degrade himself with the nihilistic spasms. But Madame Wang and her troupe, in the mixed-up mentality of Los Angeles chic, take his protest as his attempt to please them. "I like it. I like it," Madame Wang adjudges his bloodletting, "This kid's got something. Let's see if we can get him." The experience restores Lutz to his senses. He escapes the club and resolves to return to East Germany. As for the Russian invasion of America, he says, "If they take over, it's their problem."

Madame Wang's club is more explicitly related to the dread liberal society when Lutz and his friends are hired to attend a fashionable house party (at the heavenly intersection of Lotus and Seventh) on this month's theme of Street People (Last month's was The Boat People). The subject guests are actually trucked to the party like cattle. Lutz is lured into a flirtatious nonseduction by the hostess (Susan Blond) who responds to her husband's disaffection (he continually calls her "a piece of shit") by hiring Lutz to kill him. The subplot summarizes Morrissey's view of America as a shallow thrill-seeking society with idle lust and greed in place of genuine emotions and values. The party scene provides a societal equivalent to the film's key symbol: the Greek temple, standing in ludicrous isolation in Long Beach,

68

a taunting emblem of a lost, superior civilization of which only perverted parodies (of culture, freedom, and the social contract) survive at this end of Western civilization.

Into this abysmal chaos strides a character of purpose, ambition, logic, moral determination, and dedication to a selfless cause: in short, an alien. Morrissey's surrogate learns how naive and unworldly he is and how hopeless his desire for logic or order in the fallen world. Lutz was played by a young German who, like the Austrian who played Beethoven's nephew, returned to his medical studies after the film. "Both were types who controlled their own lives and I had great respect for both of them," says Morrissey. "They had a basic strength and security that kept them away from the self-destructive tendencies that seem so pervasive in young Americans. This was refreshing. Neither one had been raised in a 'liberal' environment."

Across these three comedies Morrissey seems a political alien detached from the seductive riches, liberties, and pleasures that America promises. Whether the alienation is a matter of gender, cultural dislocation, or values, the films set sensitive individuals against an amoral and tawdry social disorder. Morrissey's political comedies are films of character more than cause. "All this material, which to some people was a political cause, to me was there for humor. And also for human character. I'd never have somebody kiss someone and say 'I love you.' To me that's heavy-handed soap opera garbage. But if somebody kisses someone and says 'Oh, I forgot to clean my ears today,' then you've got a human framework and not a cliché." In all three films a political cause translates to the individual's integrity and self-control.

Although Morrissey was not involved in the polemics of the emerging American underground cinema, he shared the new cinema's insistence upon being an ethical movement foremost, and "only secondarily an aesthetic one."[8] In his difference, though, in his reactionary conservatism, Morrissey seems farther from the American movement than from the perspective taken by Jean-Luc Godard, who attacked the underground cinema in *Wind from the East:* "A cinema which thinks it is liberated. A drug cinema. A sex cinema. A cinema which claims it has been liberated by poetry, art. A cinema without taboos, except the class struggle."[9] For Morrissey, however, the taboo most vital to challenge is the progressivist myth of liberty.

Morrissey's films don't feel political because he recognized the need to provide an entertaining surface for his audience:

69

The idea of burying ideas under metaphorical action was thoroughly ingrained in me through my addiction to the films of Carol Reed, which even bear almost the same title: *Odd Man Out, The Third Man, The Man Between* – his three masterpieces – *Our Man in Havana, The Running Man,* and his similar titles, *Outcast of the Islands, The Fallen Idol.* All tell the story of the modern antihero. All take place in cities divided, usually physically (like Berlin and Vienna), all in civil war and turmoil, all concerned with antiheroes physically crossing over borders at the conclusion. This consistency of device seems so obvious but no one ever seems to see it. So I had this kind of notion of filmmaking in my mind, but comedy, not the thriller, was my surface, and I could actually hide my ideas, my themes, by calling attention to them in the title!

These political films most clearly establish the platform from which Morrissey works:

In the mind of a conservative everything good lies in an ideal reality. That reality is attainable through some kind of control. It has to be worked towards. Pandering to basest instincts, the stupid liberal says "Let it all hang out," "Do whatever you feel like doing." With three big carrots, sex, drugs, and rock and roll, they rule, they have the power, they control life under them with a much stronger hold than the Soviet dictators with their enforced puritanism ever dreamed possible. But what I think people really crave is a familial identity, not a sexual identity. Unfortunately, once you're cast adrift from custom and tradition they all want it on their own inverted terms.

4
The Costume Films

Although Morrissey is best known for his contemporary comedies – the *Flesh* trilogy and his later epics of New York street life (*Forty-Deuce, Mixed Blood, Spike of Bensonhurst*) – he also made three costume films, curious for their historical remoteness. ("Costume" seems the distinguishing term, for the *Flesh* trilogy and the "political" films are in their own way period pieces.) Two are schlock entertainments: *Blood for Dracula* (1973; released as *Andy Warhol's Dracula*) and *Flesh for Frankenstein* (1973; released as *Andy Warhol's Frankenstein*). As Morrissey told Melton Dawes, "We're injecting our style into a formula film."[1] The "style" was jocular: "I don't think it really matters whether a film is photographed to look fantastic or whether it looks really awful. If you come away from the film and you have had a somewhat amusing time, you've seen something that approaches a good film."[2] The third costume film is a full-blown "European" art movie, *Beethoven's Nephew* (1985), with sumptuous Vienna location shooting, a rich score, and operatic performances. It may seem perverse to group the classy Beethoven with the broadly comic Dracula and Frankenstein. But like other forms of adversity, film criticism makes strange bedfellows. Despite their difference in genre and "brow" (the low and middle-high respectively), the three works are consistent.

Their period accoutrements notwithstanding, the three films are comedies. As Morrissey told *Newsweek* in 1974, "I've always made anti-erotic comedies. Sex is the best subject for comedy because it's so silly. I ridicule it because people try to use it as some sort of cure-all. I ridicule violence because it's another sacred cow today."[3] In the costume films he also ridicules the pretentions of historical cinema and the romantic myths of genius, whether artistic or scientific.

Paradoxically, these three costume works may be Morrissey's most personal films. As his contemporary films center upon current concerns, he seemed inclined to restrain his own voice. Indeed during the *Flesh* and *Heat* years he made both an ethic and aesthetic out of not imposing himself upon his material. But in the period films the distancing by costume and by genre conventions seems to have encouraged more personal utterance. He could be more open in apparent fabrications than in his ostensibly "recorded" contemporary works.

Both horror films open with a leisurely pan behind the credits to distinguish the *made* world from the *natural* world. In *Frankenstein,* the presumably innocent children are obscured by the baron's lab apparatus, as they eviscerate, then guillotine, a doll. They are obviously chips off the old block. The next scene shows the children and their mother in white, drawn in a pony cart through a pastoral landscape. The children are not as innocent as the shot suggests. In the ordering of the scenes, the children are identified with suspect science before they appear in the idyllic nature. They share the baron's association with the unnatural "science." Later, in their room, we see a cage with two mechanical birds. In *Dracula,* beside the opening titles, the count paints an artificial color and life over his pallor – another association of the man-made with the unnatural.

All three films express Morrissey's major concerns. Powerful heroes fail to achieve a full self or life – *because* they have too much power or freedom. Sexual exploitation and its failure remain dominant themes, with physical possession the primary mode of the characters' relationships. Baron Frankenstein and his sister are destroyed by their unbridled sexual freedom, Dracula by his eternal need for (that rarity) virgin's blood, and Beethoven by the unbounded authority his society gives him in reward for his genius. All three are cases of fatally licensed appetite.

But a more private theme may unite the three costume dramas. We find a clue in their release titles: *Warhol's Dracula, Warhol's Frankenstein, Beethoven's Nephew* (though in the first two cases the titles were changed by the distributors). All three carry the idea of possession. In all three titles – and plots – the master possesses his apprentice through his work. Morrissey has often been interested in the theme of "people trying to take over other people as substitute lives for themselves." The legendary vampire and the mad scientist share this with Beethoven's historical domination of his nephew (indeed, of his entire family).

The strictly commercial ploy of identifying Morrissey's film with his more famous producer points up this continuing theme of human possession. Though Warhol had nothing to do with either film, they are often included in *his* canon, not Morrissey's, as recently as Carter Ratcliff's 1983 monograph: "With his versions of *Dracula* (1974) and *Frankenstein* (1974), Warhol made a bid for marketplace success. Although they did moderately well at the box office, these movies have an afterlife only as cult objects. Their appeal even when new may have owed as much to Warhol's aura as to their scariness, which is not convincing"[4] – nor intended! *Flesh, Heat, Trash,* and *Women in Revolt* were also "Warhol's" in ad name only.

But Morrissey has never complained at Warhol's being credited for Morrissey's films. On the contrary, he lauds Warhol as a benefactor content to let others achieve their own desires: "In everything to do with film, Andy always did whatever I asked him to do. His ideas never went beyond 'Why don't you use this person?' In ninety percent of the cases I didn't think they were right and I didn't use them and he didn't mind. I was completely free. He paid the bills and I did what I wanted to." But even if the possessive titles don't reflect on Morrissey's career, in these films he expresses a sensitivity to the disadvantaged junior, failed by a master responsible for his charge's fulfillment. Morrissey denies this leaning: "I'm sensitive to all the characters equally. I have no favorites. In an immoral world no one is better or worse than any other."

Even if Morrissey does not consciously reflect on his situation with Warhol, one consistent theme across the three films is the interdependence of servant and master. In *Beethoven's Nephew* a ward is suppressed by a famous superior. In the two schlock horror films, dominated servants rebel. In the first, Otto revolts by disastrously assuming his master's misunderstanding of sexuality. Dracula's servant remains loyal and self-sacrificing to the end, but there is a rebellion by the irreverent peasant. Similarly, Beethoven's nephew delays moving toward independence until it is too late for him to escape, even after he is freed by his famous uncle's death. The servant's hunger to break free is balanced by his need for discipline and for his master's support. The flawed master needs his assistant for the simple basics of survival.

Morrissey does not remember Warhol as any kind of master; quite the contrary:

As a presence or some kind of figure in my consciousness, he never really, I think, existed. Andy was a very timid, flimsy character, a person I had to tell what to do, and who really needed someone to guide him, even to speak for him. I was totally controlling all the films, the one thing the Factory was really famous for. I controlled almost every other area except his paintings. I managed all his business affairs, including real estate, and owned fifty percent of all the films.

73

I don't think the extent to which Andy depended on others has ever been fully realized.

With his total control over his films and his sympathy for all three monsters, Morrissey rather than Warhol identifies with the master characters in the stories. "These three characters are looking for some sort of system that makes life work, some policy of behavior that makes sense," Morrissey says, "But they're doomed to never find it, doomed to go on living under the liberal 'go to hell and do whatever you want' tyranny." The fact that all three master/monster figures are Germanic is especially significant. "To a non-German, Germans always are characterized as people who want to control life, make it orderly, believe that it can be improved or perfected. And paradoxically, they are the world's greatest romantics. I go to Germany a great deal and see it still very much there in its young people. I don't see it elsewhere."

This theme of the fatal power of the romantic figure grows more explicit in the course of the three films. The baron, the count, and the prototypal romantic composer all cut a larger-than-life swath through our imagination. All three are men of extraordinary (even superhuman) power. Morrissey's point is that they destroy themselves with their own freedom. All three heroes are cursed with power or genius: they lose their will, are isolated by their abuse of others, and are tormented by their inner voids. The baron and the count anticipate the negative consequence Morrissey spelled out more fully in his Beethoven story, where the extreme license granted the romantic will, or the individualistic ego, ends the coherent social and moral order. As Morrissey says, "Beethoven was a personification of the fictitious lunacy in the Frankenstein and Dracula characters and it was all historically true." Nonetheless, all three monster geniuses pursue an idealized reality that exists far away: the ideal musical forms beyond the deaf Beethoven's grasp, Dracula's virgin blood in far-off Italy, and Frankenstein's classical ideal beyond his enervated German stock.

In this light, the three costume films dramatize the source of modern anomie chronicled in the *Flesh* trilogy. In the contemporary films, a passive figure drifts into contamination by the corrupt modern world. In the costume films, the prole hero confronts an equally destructive figure of superior power and social authority. The debility of the contemporary heroes can be attributed to the mythologizing of the individual ego and its rights to untrammeled indulgence. The Beethoven romantic's unrestrained assertion leads down to the empty and crumbling ego of the Dallesandro characters. Or, as Paul Zimmerman observed, where Morrissey had "studied a new kind of zombie – the freaked-out neo-Bohemians of the '60s" in *Trash* and a vampirish or "predatory relationship between a Hollywood mother and daughter" in *Heat*, in *Frankenstein* "he reorchestrates his vision of a sexually sick, unfeeling and manipulative society within the literal conventions of the horror genre."[5] With striking prescience, Parker Tyler found in Hollywood's early hallucinogenic cinema, such as Roger Corman's *The Trip* (1967), traditional stereotypes from the Dracula and Frankenstein horrors.[6]

Certainly Morrissey considered the two horror films to be consistent with his earlier work, as he explained in a 1973 interview:

> We're trying to make movies in a style that's commensurate with the way people live their lives today. For instance, before the war, there were moral codes, a certain guilty conscience about things, there was more of a form to life itself. Now life is formless, aimless, people aren't tormented by guilt and they're not bound by moral codes. You can make a movie about that subject, but it's a different thing to make a movie in that frame of mind.[7]

The schlock subject of the horrors was consistent with Morrissey's aversion to "important titles. They're shop-worn and abused. Also we'd rather make films that, hopefully, critics would be forced *not* to review."[8] The slumming titles were another end run around judgmental critics, directly to engage an audience expecting to be amused.

Flesh for Frankenstein (1973)

In Morrissey's version, the mad doctor Baron Frankenstein (Udo Kier) is married to his sister, Katrin (Monique Van Vooren). They live with their two children (Carla Mancini, Marco Liofredi) in the obligatory castle. With his faithful servant Otto (Arno Juerging), the baron attempts to synthesize a couple who will perpetuate the ideals of ancient Greece, now to be found only among the Serbian race. This ambition is as Germanic as manic. His female creation (Dalila Di Lazzaro) is complete. For Morrissey, "Always the problem is with the male, never the female." To complete his male, Frankenstein wants the primitive head of a man of lustful energies, "a man who wants to make love to anything," but with the perfect Serbian nose. Always Morrissey finds a pursuit for some lost, classical ideal, however debased in the contemporary quest. (So, too, Morrissey's Dracula wistfully recalls his youth, when he would ride out in his carriage with his governess and "the streets were filled with" virgins.)

But the scientist mistakes which of two brothel visitors would serve his

75

The unnatural creations (Srdjan Zelenovic and Dalila Di Lazzaro) are examined by Otto (Arno Juerging) and Baron Frankenstein (Udo Kier) in *Flesh for Frankenstein*.

needs. Instead of the lusty Nicholas (Joe Dallesandro), the baron takes the head of the peasant's cerebral friend, Sasha (Srdjan Zelenovic), whose chastity inclines him to the monastery. Consequently the baron fails to achieve his creatures' animal mating, which would have been the Dallesandro character's specialty. While the baron finishes his specimens, his lustful wife/sister hires Nicholas as her butler/stud. She betrays him when he threatens to expose the baron. When she claims her reward – the sexual use of the male monster – he squeezes her to death. Meanwhile Otto, naively emulating his master's sexual activity, disembowels maid Olga (Liu Bosisio) and the female specimen. Symptomatically, he confuses the woman's wound with her sex organs for his penetration. When the male monster recognizes his friend Nicholas, he murders the baron, then plucks out his own guts, preferring death over life as a mutant. At the end, the baron's two enigmatic children approach the captive Dallesandro bent upon resuming their father's experiments.

Not content just to parody the genre, Morrissey develops the central

76

psychological aspects of his legend. From the *Frankenstein* lore, Morrissey singles out the idea of sexual displacement. As Walter Evans has demonstrated, the Frankenstein story is about the unnatural urge to find an alternative to sex.[9] "Otto" is an especially appropriate name for the assistant in autoeroticism. And his master is not just capable of superhuman science but incapable of normal sexuality. He is also the Barren Frankenstein.

Morrissey locates the myth in his familiar target of sexual license. The baroness reveals that both their parents were irresponsible libertines who neglected their children except with negative example. So their aberrant sexuality has ancestral roots. The baron was further traumatized by the sight of naked women in a brothel during his student days. He was "shocked" to see the women's overdeveloped breasts and body hair and their lascivious movements. His horror of the flesh parallels the obsession with it in *Flesh*. Although he lives with his sister as man and wife, their two children are more likely illegitimate than the fruit of incest. Characteristic of Morrissey's frisky perspective, our choice here is between the illicit and the taboo. The baron shows no sexual interest in his sister/wife, nor jealousy of her sexual use of her new servant and the monster. That is, his marriage is a parody and a denial of the conventional relationship that validates sexuality and reproduction. Typical of Morrissey's vision, the false marriage is defined not by abstinence but by a perverse liberty. As in Evans's summary of the Frankenstein story, "In order to lead a normal, healthy life, Henry Frankenstein...must learn to deal safely and normally with the 'secret of life,' however revolting, however evil, however it might seem to frighten and actually threaten pure, virgin womanhood."[10]

Out of his own sexual drive, the baron reaches inside his female creature to fondle her innards and waxes orgasmic over her interior inventory: "spleen – kidneys – gall-bladder – liver." This is not a conventional love scene; there is no skin-deep love here. He enters her wound with his penis for, as he tells Otto in one of the great schlock lines of cinema, "To know death, Otto, you have to fuck life – in the gall bladder." Morrissey intended the line to parody Bertolucci's *Last Tango in Paris,* specifically the Marlon Brando character's line, "You won't be able to be free of that feeling of being alone until you look death right in the face.... Until you go right up into the ass of death – right up his ass – till you find a womb of fear."[11] Morrissey considers Bertolucci's film "the worst kind of soap opera dressed up with these pretentious allusions, its self-proclaimed importance."

Morrissey satirizes the hypocrisy of the righteous. While acting out his passion, the baron orders Otto ("You filthy thing") not to watch. But the baron shares Otto's voyeurism. When the baron spies on his wife/sister's sex, her schlurping kisses of Nicholas's armpit express the baron's nauseated perception. Lacking the master's restraint, Otto's sexual activity destroys both the maid and the specimen. In the same hypocritical spirit, the baron decorously tapes the genitals and anuses of his corpses. Otto fastidiously retapes the female's crotch before he enters her stomach wound. Dallesandro's libidinous peasant is ethically superior to the others in their hypocrisy.

These tensions are played off in a cheeky version of family sitcom. The baron's wife actually complains: "Never any time for us. Always running off to that stupid laboratory." In both horror films the master and his faithful servant bicker and nag as if a comedic married couple. The baron scolds Otto as the baroness scolds the children for their messy lab/room. The mistress's exploitation of the Dallesandro character also anticipates the class tension in *Dracula*. Shocked to see him disporting himself with peasant girls, she summons him in to scold or to fire. But, her lust at odds with her moral pretenses, she instead takes him as a lover.

At the producers' suggestion, the film was shot in the Grander Guignol of 3-D. Morrisey "thought it was a ridiculous idea and therefore, it appealed to me. That's all."[12] But he took full advantage of the technology. In the credit sequence the exaggerated depth pushes the baron's lab equipment forward as a threatening but quavering machinery.[13] Morrissey also exploits the shock/schlock values of the 3-D thrust into the audience, after the prototypal *House of Wax* (1953). Aptly, the first major objects thrust out at us are seminal vesicles. This form of ejaculation turns the depth device into an alternative to sexual entry. That is, Morrissey's filmmaking technology parallels the baron's medical experiments. In the next scene some tumbling apples (Eden Reds?) bring the family's innocent picnic into the peasants' alfresco fornication. The 3-D device suggests an onanist parallel to spilled fruit. If Michael Snow's *Wavelength* (1967) is (among other readings) the camera's sexual penetration of a room, Morrissey's 3-D screws the audience – or posits an ejaculatory alternative.

The 3-D thrusts also parallel the baron's unconventional sexuality in confronting man's elemental physicality. Hence several shots in which cadavers' feet loom into the audience, the threatening pincers with which the baron advances against Sasha, the guts that tumble out of several bodies, the baron's spurting blood, and the climactic dangling of his guts when Sasha drives a spear through him. These 3-D effects served the function of "ridiculing the violence in other films," Morrissey told the American Film Institute.[14] He was not being disingenuous. For in any film of such pronounced conventions, the film does not refer the viewer back to reality but to other films of its genre.

For an antithesis to the shock rhetoric of 3-D, Morrissey gives us formal dinner scenes at such a wide table that it takes fifteen seconds to pan across. This establishes the family's respectable false front. The societal norm is represented by the lateral stretch of the screen; the 3-D thrusts represent the violating irruptions of the unrestrained ego. The emphatic attack by belfry bats colloquially defines the family egotism as madness.

The open-ended conclusion (a familiar twist in horror films that long preceded critical concepts of closure and suture) posits an extension of the baron's schemes. Almost wordless, the children watch everything with a sinister seriousness. They later discover a separate throbbing heart and lungs in a closet. The children's monstrousness derives from their parents' separation of mind from body (literally, in Sasha's decapitation), when man's physical nature escapes rational control. As the children have inherited their parents' and grandparents' malevolent liberties, they too will treat people as sexual objects with interchangeable parts. They already have a fish tank, a miniature of their father's large tank in which he preserves the female specimen.

Morrissey's *Frankenstein* is a parable about the destruction wrought by unbridled sexuality. The baroness's lust may bring her the vitality of the peasant, but never sated, she craves the better-endowed zombie. For this she is suffocated. That is, the inevitable consequence of her power is fatally to lose control. The baron's lust is even worse than hers, for he craves a creative power that would transcend sex. As his scientific knowledge frees him from the sexual function of creation, it leads him to destructive perversion. The couple personify the perversity of unrestrained sexuality. Both have their higher pretenses, the baron to scientific discovery and his sister to aestheticism: "I have always looked for beauty. As a matter of fact, I insist on it." As with Maurice Braddell's speech in *Flesh*, "even ideas that I am sympathetic to can be corrupted by license." The license of Frankenstein and his sister undermines the ideal of sexual freedom.

The baron's doom is sealed when all three women are piled up as corpses. When Morrissey intercuts the delivery of the baroness's and the female specimen's corpses, the women seem parallel instances of death-in-life, creatures whose sexuality outlived their proper spirit. In their sexual destruction, one by smothering and the other by gutting (that is, the lungs and the heart again), both the breath/spirit and the flesh reveal their mortality. With woman reduced to lust, the entire natural process of procreation and fertility has been corrupted. So Morrissey frames the film with scenes of the precocious children assuming their legacy of sadistic and antinatural science.

In contrast, Dallesandro portrays his most positive figure since *Flesh*. His

American accent (the only one in the film, as in *Dracula*) opposes him to the European aristocracy caricatured in the film. He embodies American vitality, democracy, and – in his persistent fidelity to his beheaded friend – a rare unselfishness. He is also identified with nature, not just for his various field work but in the brothel, where a small lizard scampers across the familiar landscape of Dallesandro's derriere. The baroness might have redeemed herself had she escaped with and to the natural sexuality of the Dallesandro character. Instead she betrays him to her brother and as reward lays mortal claim to the apparatus of the monster. In contrast, the baron's servant has no independent abilities or knowledge to strengthen their relationship. Otto can only (at best) do what he is told. Specifically, he lacks the sense and energy of normal sexuality, the very salvation the peasant might have provided the baroness. Here, as in *Dracula*, Dallesandro is cast as a conveyor of sexual energy with moral and political force. But as his sexuality renders him vulnerable, the film's true moral center rests in the integrity of the Sasha character instead. That celibate is also doomed, for the corrupted world of sexual license allows no place for innocence.

Blood for Dracula (1973)

Having run out of Romanian virgins to provide his life-sustaining blood, Count Dracula (Udo Kier) buries his sister and is moved by his faithful manservant Anton (Arno Juerging) to the good Catholic promise of Italy. The Di Fioris, an aristocratic family bankrupted by gambling, is eager to provide a virgin wife. But their two likeliest prospects are both having affairs with the family's handyman, Mario Balato (Joe Dallesandro). The beauties, Saphiria (Dominique Darel) and Rubinia (Stefania Casini), in order, become Dracula's hench-vamps even though his system rejects their postvirgin blood. When the count's vampirism is discovered, the handyman rapes the fourteen-year-old sister, Perla (Silvia Dionisio), theoretically to protect her. The oldest sister, Esmerelda (Milena Vukotic), a spinster since an earlier engagement was broken off, provides Dracula with the virgin blood he needs. With the marquis in London, the marquise and Otto kill each other. Mario drives a wooden stake through the vampire's heart. The once sober, now crazed, Esmeralda joins the count in death by leaping onto his stake, in a Gothic parody of phallic union.

The film infuses the highly conventionalized genre with Morrissey's calculated casualness. For example, though the daughters often seem to be inconsistent in their behavior, alternately sympathetic victims and libidinous monsters, sometimes cute and sometimes nasty, they serve Morrissey's sense of realistic characterization:

> Even in these absurd situations ... psychological nuances appear. ... I think they approach reality a little more. People are really capable of being many different things. If it's all written down for the actors and they read their parts in advance and they figure who they are and what kind of person they're going to play, they play that kind of person all the way through the script. When it's informal and free, they can be lustful here and childish there and sympathetic here and not so sympathetic in other scenes. I found it very useful as far as characterization goes.[15]

In this sense Morrissey stayed in the Factory aesthetic: "The aesthetic was one of the performers; it wasn't letting the camera run without stopping," he says. "That was the form; but the content was ... the record on film of people's personalities in depth and in some richness."[16] Morrissey adds resonance to a genre uninterested in characterization.

The film also contrasts two master–servant relationships. In one, the selfless Anton faithfully serves Count Dracula. In the other, the self-indulgent handyman exploits the sexuality of three of his master's daughters. The difference is not just between selflessness and selfishness; it is also between the former's location in myth and the latter's roots in social reality. Everything in Anton's nature comes from the never-never-land of vampire lore. The handyman's activity is rooted in Dallesandro's contemporary associations, his speech in the Marxist mythology. The lore and the rhetoric are equally artificial. But like the master–servant relationships central to the other two costume films, both here are characterized by a mix of erotic service and tension.

Morrissey also develops a consistent theme involving language. Perhaps the most striking element in Morrissey's casualness is his polyglot of accent. Virtually every conversation rings incongruous. The Marquis Di Fiori (Vittorio De Sica) establishes the expected norm of Italian accent. But while his daughters speak various forms of Italian English, his wife (Maxime McKendry) is purely British. As the family's second-generation handyman, Dallesandro personifies anachronism with his untempered modern New York accent and colloquialisms ("Am I gonna see you two latah?" "So what's he doin' wit' you two hooers?").

This aberrant language underlines the conventional nature of the genre by denying any pretense to verisimilitude. Morrissey exposes the falseness of historical pretense in period fiction. In fiction the subject is not the period depicted but the period in which the work is made. For the author's vision is inevitably rooted in – and focused on – his own times. Teasing the notion that language serves any consistent reality, Morrissey deploys it as just a convention. When Anton advises his master to go to Italy for a reliable supply of "wheregins," Dracula at first does not understand him. "Wheregins?" he asks. Thereafter Anton has no trouble pronouncing the *v*. More pointedly, the handyman is referred to by a variety of names. The marquise refers to him once as Balato and later as Damato. One daughter calls him Mario, another Lucino. This suggests the peasant's anonymity to the aristocracy. The handyman quarrels with Anton over a telling misunderstanding of name: "I'm no one's 'servant.' I'm a 'worker' here." The archaic aristocrat assumes that "worker and servant are the same."

The marquis makes nomenclature a theme when he muses on the musicality of the visitor's name: "Dracula? The sound is intriguing. Three syllables – Dra-cue-la. I think I like that name." The irony is that the marquis fixes on the speculative associations of that name, oblivious to the meanings that the vampire myth has established. "There are wine tasters and there are name tasters," the marquis avers, confident that "Dracula" betokens someone "aged in the wood, of excellent culture."[7] The talkative marquis seems to valorize the myth when he approves Dracula's name for combining "just the right amount of Orient and Occident, of reality and fantasy."

The marquis parallels Count Dracula in futilely trying to sustain a traditional respectability against an antipathetic modernity. There is also a kindred romanticism in the marquis's poetry: "Flowers that are too cultivated lose some of their *parfum*. They wither too quickly." He even shares the view that sex damages the appearance, saying, "Early marriage tends to ruin the complexion." Both old men have survived into alien times. Though the marquis adores live flowers and the count dead ones, both live in an arid and denatured world. Of course, the aristocrat's name, Di Fiori, alludes to the transient beauty of flowers (and, fugitively, of pride).

The marquis's three airy monologues on Dracula's name contrast the prolonged scenes that establish the count's tragic corporeality. Having tasted the impure blood of the two middle sisters in order, the count is shown graphically retching. His blood vomit, quite beyond the conventions both of the genre and of taste, serves to establish the count's physical agony in contrast to the marquis's airiness and the women's trivial sensuality. This point also justifies the risible shot of Dracula lapping off the floor the blood of Perla's defloration. Even when Dracula finds prized virgin blood, it is in the form of refuse in which no one else has any interest. Earlier, Anton had brought Dracula a loaf of bread that he had placed in the gutter outside of the tavern, to soak up the blood of a twelve-year-old (i.e., possibly virgin) girl, conveniently hurt in a traffic accident. Finally, when Mario destroys Dracula by chopping off his limbs one at a time, first the arms (aptly if not disarmingly disarming Dracula), then each leg, the duration and gore may be comic but, like the blood-vomit, they express the count's enemy, his physicality. Although he is an immortal spirit, he is locked in a body with mortal appetite.

Both aristocrats contrast the handyman's physical substance and prowess. Mario's superior strength translates to substance. In contrast to the count's lack of reflection in mirrors, Mario is shown combing his hair in a mirror, which also reveals Saphiria and Rubinia having sex with each other after having had Mario. When the characters appear in the mirror they seem less substantial than Dracula, who, as a vampire, is a physical presence without a reflection. Where Dracula thrives on a woman's purity, Mario thrives on her corruption. Morrissey shares his monster's rue at the loss of values and self-control, though they have different reasons for regretting the virtual obsolescence of the virgin in the modern world. So undervalued is chastity that in the tavern the virgin (and chaste) Esmerelda is referred to as "a real tramp" because her long engagement was broken off.

As the film assumes its audience's understanding of genre, the viewer's complicity is first summoned when the opening pan establishes the count applying makeup, then freezes on a gaslight flickering in a mirror, in which the vampire is not reflected. The climactic revelation in that pan is what is *not* seen. Later Mario discovers the truth about Dracula when he finds a coffin empty. Both moments are based on the tension between the substantial and the phantom, with the latter the more significant.

One incidental comic scene supports major motifs of the plot and fore-shadows the aristocrats' defeat by the peasant. In the tavern, Polish film director Roman Polanski plays a peasant who tricks Anton in a gambling variation on the mirror motif.[18] The game was Polanski's idea, but it fits brilliantly. Anton loses the bet when he is unable to imitate Polanski's every gesture – specifically, spitting out the wine that he earlier seemed to drink. The scene establishes the gap between the peasant and the aristocrat and the peasant's greater savvy. The ordinary mortal succeeds through living a version of mirror behavior and by being in control of the red liquid he imbibes. Evoking the handyman's Marxism, the Polanski character's first remark is that he and his mates are still owed payment for four years of carrying the Di Fiori family's manure.

It is rather striking that Morrissey cast two prominent directors in the

Before the gambling at the inn: Anton (Arno Juerging) and (third from left)
Roman Polanski in *Blood for Dracula.*

film. Where Warhol preferred to associate with and use celebrities, Morrissey preferred unknown performers. "I prefer the luxury of working with
unknowns," Morrissey told the American Film Institute. But in the industry,
he admits that conventional wisdom says, "You *need* a star. It's not a luxury
to have a star.... you're more fortunate to be able to use whoever you feel
like using."[9] On the other hand, he also was fascinated by the existential
frisson when an actor stepped out of his role. His interest in the tension
between performer and role is as apparent in his casting of two directors
here as in his earlier use of transvestite performers.

That tension invites the contrast between the two directors who perform
here. De Sica has a double persona as a lead in commercial romances and
as the essential neorealist director of *The Bicycle Thief, Miracle in Milan*
and *Umberto D.* Polanski has a similar double image as a European-
American and as an absurdist/horror director. Taken together, the former
registers as an impotent romantic aristocrat, the latter as a potent pragmatic

In *Blood for Dracula*, the Marxist (Joe Dallesandro) entertains the lady Rubinia (Stefanie Carsini).

peasant. The former is victim of the vanity of the mirror, the latter its master in a playful gamble on its duplication. But as two directors playing characters, they register as both inside and outside the fiction of the film – indeed, as Morrissey seems both inside and outside his genre. He plays along with its form but subverts its spirit.

Much of the comedy involves social satire. As the inn owner says of the Di Fiori family, "Oh, I'm sure they are religious; they have a very nice house." That "religious" is a sham respectability, not virtue. For his part, Dracula is leery of Italy for its lack of virgins and its excess of salad oil. In what is perhaps the film's most pointed satire, Morrissey parallels Dracula's vital need for virgin's blood to the marquise's avid hunger for "new money," which exposes her daughters to the danger of the count. Knowing his prey, the first thing Anton tells the marquise is about Dracula's wealth. So for her, "Count Dracula may not seem like the ideal husband but he comes from a very good family." She coaxes her reluctant daughters with predictions of an early and profitable widowhood. As Mario points out, the marquise is as culpable as Dracula, for being so "stupid and money crazy" in trying to marry off her daughters.

85

Mario has a red hammer and sickle painted on the wall over his bed. But his Marxist rhetoric is as shallow as that painted slogan. True, the Marxist democrat may have history on his side when he dismisses his rival, the count: "Right now he's a disgusting person with money. After the revolution he'll be a disgusting person without money." But Mario's Marxism is another freedom that turns out to be tyranny. He flaunts an alternative mythology, akin to the privilege assumed by the aristocrats and the literary conventions exercised in vampire lore. Indeed, the political rhetoric seems as incongruous as Dallesandro's accent in a native Italian peasant. It is as if the only accent Dallesandro has chosen to perform when he stepped out of Brooklyn into an Italian film was the de rigeur politics! In the same ironic spirit, the two loose sisters allude to the sensationalized politics of *Bitter Rice* (1949) when they bare their bosoms in the field, pretending to be peasants. (Indeed Morrissey's shift from predominantly male nudity to female in his Italian horrors may be donning a foreign market accent, after his breakthrough male exposure in the *Flesh* trilogy.)

Mario's Marxism is undermined by the brutal way he treats his lovers. In one scene, under his vaunted hammer and sickle, he slaps Rubinia and forces her to fellate him. Little wonder that she is quickly converted to Dracula's service when he sucks her neck on the bathroom floor. In another scene, Mario withdraws from raping Rubinia when he seems put off by her confession of love. That is, not only can sex and love no longer coexist, sex has become a barrier to the possibility of love. Here the love drives out the sex; the failing is mutual. Mario's communism satirizes the political palaver Morrissey kept hearing in Italy: directors like Bertolucci and the actors "talk seriously about communism. . . . they have an example like Yugoslavia right on their borders and they actually talk very seriously about how wonderful communism will be. So I thought it was silly."[20]

Still, Mario's Marxist clichés are preferable to both aristocratic alternatives, the Di Fioris' financial and moral bankruptcy and the vampire's eternal thirst for blood. Indeed, Mario's exploitation of the first two sisters proves less destructive than their violation by Dracula. We may even accept Mario's rape to protect Perla from the Count: "You should lose that virginity of yours before he gets to you," he advises. But Mario's motive is undercut by a large tapestry depicting a country hunt. It suggests that the Marxist is simply replacing one predatory politic with another. The marquise's response to the rape is wrongheaded. "You're just an employee," she says. "How dare you put my daughter in such an unfortunate position?" In both Mario and the marquise, Morrissey satirizes the self-indulgent's rationalizing.

Dracula has his innings too. Esmerelda's devotion to Dracula represents a fulfillment that her spinsterish gentility could never have provided. Morrissey does not show her union with Dracula, implying it is too pure and personal; however, Dracula's union with the two coarse daughters is shown, the first in the bedroom, the second in the toilet. In both blood-takings we see, the women reach orgasm under the count's sucking at their necks. When the count retches up their impure blood, the life-sucking monster becomes a sympathetic moral force, physically suffering from the women's corruption: "My body can't take this treatment any more," he says. "The blood of these whores is killing me. I just want my coffin to sleep in." In his corrupted world, sex means death for the great romantic hero. For all the vampire's evil, here he exposes the more corrupt aristocracy. As one sister defends the other's willingness to lie to marry him, "It's her responsibility, to marry someone like him. She's only doing what she was brought up to do." (That last phrase is all the more felicitous for coming hard upon the count's retching in the preceding scene.)

The woman's excuse may apply equally to the handyman's sexual and political liberation. As he climbs the highborn woman's body with kisses, he whispers Red nothings: the aristocrat's "days are numbered, I'm telling you"; the aristocrats are all "sick and rotten" like the pallid, feeble count: "The only future is socialism. . . . All you got is a title to put in front of your names. And someday that's not going to count either. You'll be on the bottom." And so the lovers lash themselves into sexual ecstasy with his revolutionary rhetoric – and her plans to shop in Paris.

The handyman ultimately finds his Marxism less effective than his vampire lore. When the wooden stake dispatches the vampire, his fall also signifies the fall of the aristocracy, as the handyman says, "He lives off other people. He's no good to anyone. He never was." The film closes with the handyman escorting the youngest daughter into the house and closing the gate against us. By driving out the vampire/aristocrat, the New York City peasant has assumed mastery in the aristocrat's dilapidated house. This is not an unequivocally happy ending. It establishes the new power of the vulgar and a trivial self-indulgence, contrasted to the archaic class of the aristocracy and the passion of the vanquished count.

In *Dracula,* Morrissey elaborates on the political association of bloodsucking. Even in F. W. Murnau's *Nosferatu* (1923), the Dracula figure was less a sexual threat than an image of the (inferably Jewish) alien sucking the blood of a sleeping, innocent nation. In Morrissey's version of peasant besting vampire, the worker overthrows the sick and rotting aristocracy. In terms of metacinema it may also represent another ascent to new power:

New York neorealism supplants the classical political cinema when Vittorio De Sica plays an impotent romantic whose family is saved, albeit compromised, by the virile New Yorker.

Beethoven's Nephew (1985)

In *Beethoven's Nephew,* Morrissey reached both a new level of technical sophistication and a peak in his personal expression. This film has none of the compromises of an independent's film; on the contrary, it has the polish and resonance of a European art movie.[21]

In some respects the film seems to follow upon the success of Peter Shaffer's exposé of Mozart's vulgar character, *Amadeus,* successfully filmed by Milos Forman. But Morrissey had begun researching his Beethoven project before Forman's film appeared. The adaptation of Luigi Magnani's novel *Beethoven's Nephew* had gone through several screenplays and production plans before Morrissey was brought in by Jean-Jacques Fourgeaud, who produced *Forty-Deuce.* Morrissey rewrote the screenplay (collaborating with Mathieu Carrière, who appears in the film as Archduke Rodolphe). His script moved closer to Beethoven's conversation books and to the public knowledge that Beethoven was an extraordinarily nasty person, who admitted moral responsibility to no one. "An utterly untamed personality," Goethe called him in 1812, as kindly as he could. To Morrissey, "Beethoven was pure Molière, a character of lunacy and exaggeration, not the Shakespearean hero that the Germans now pretend. That was widely known during his lifetime." To prove he was presenting the historical Beethoven, Morrissey included in the film's first press kits a dense selection of excerpts from the conversation books, Beethoven's letters, and contemporary reports. The material was generally ignored.

Morrissey's film reveals the tyranny of Ludwig van Beethoven (Wolfgang Reichmann) over his young nephew, Karl (Dietmar Prinz), during the last eleven years of the composer's life. The film contrasts the maestro's magnificent achievement in music with his astonishingly brutish behavior, what was, in his brother's words, Beethoven's "almost total incapacity to have normal relationships with other people." The film displays the historical Beethoven of petty greed, paranoia, unbridled egotism, and possessive jealousy, who is yet pathetic for his obsessive stranglehold on his nephew. "I always saw the nephew as the adult, with the strength to withstand the eleven years of torture, and Beethoven as the spoiled child throwing tantrums," says Morrissey, who respects the nephew's strength. "He married and had five daughters," he says. "They said their father was a good man but he would never talk about his awful uncle. My sympathy was never with the nephew, because I knew he was the winner in the contest. I wasn't against him – he wasn't bad – but to a romantic like Beethoven he represented something bad." Beethoven is the typical Morrissey libertine: given unrestrained license in his own life, he seeks total control over others.

But Morrissey's point runs deeper than the demystification of one composer's family. At the heart of the film is the paradox that the negative energies of Beethoven's strangling love for his nephew are the power behind his major compositions. In Morrissey's view, the emotionalism new to Beethoven's late quartets and to the choral finale of his Ninth Symphony was the expression of new resources that Beethoven discovered through his love for his nephew. "When Beethoven looks at his nephew, his emotions are not spoken but heard on the soundtrack, the emotions of the idealized music," Morrissey says. "The music is not mundane, certainly not sexual. It's the romantic ideal. But to the liberal, an attractive young face is only there for sexual reasons. For me an idealized appearance is a metaphor for a previous kind of harmony." The film locates the deepest spring of artistic emotion in passion that can destroy both the subject and the object.

Indeed, as the European romantic movement in the arts derives from this new focus in Beethoven, Morrissey exposes a human cost to more than just the single eccentric composer. Morrissey challenges the entire romantic movement in the arts. The egotism and license afforded both by the romantic ethic and by the power of Beethoven's celebrity enabled him to do unconscionable things to the people closest to him (and be rude to his casual acquaintances), without fear of restraint or retribution. The man of genius ruined the lives of his brothers, daughter-in-law, nephew, and even himself through his wasting will. In a comic miniature of this theme, the headmaster accepts the deaf Beethoven's mishearing when he reduces "Claire Antoinette" to "Clarinet," in effect accepting Beethoven's reduction of a human being to an instrument.

Morrissey's reflections on the dangers of romanticism are especially pertinent to the American independent film scene. Morrissey's film aesthetic was at least in large measure a reaction against the romanticism of Stan Brakhage – and to the poetic cinema most fervidly espoused by Jonas Mekas. Morrissey especially abjured the fantastical interests of the visionary cinema, preferring the social bonds of morality and comprehensible communication. For Brakhage, the social reality is only fodder for his filmic manipulation, in the service of his private imagination. Morrissey subordinates his own inner life to observing the sources of his subjects' behavior. In this light, Beethoven stands for the aberrant personal art that denies social, aesthetic, or moral obligation.[22]

Finally, there is the irony that this master creator of art should have felt driven to such cruel lengths because he could not achieve the more universal and simple creation of his own child. In this respect Morrissey's Beethoven is a pathetic giant like his other two unnatural monsters, Dracula and Frankenstein. Beethoven, too, tampers with the natural order of life and death when he tears his nephew away from the boy's mother. All three monsters are superhuman impotents.

It is tempting to infer that Beethoven's neurosis and anxiety are sexually based. The maestro's stranglehold on his nephew is clearest in his rage at the boy's normal sexual development. He accuses his elderly housekeeper (Erna Korhel) of having designs upon young Karl, suspects the boarding school of immoral sexual activity, bodily extracts Karl from a young maid and begs the boy's actress-mistress, Leonore (Nathalie Baye), to surrender him. A hallway of trophy horns makes Beethoven look like the traditional cuckold when he storms off to interrupt Karl's sex with the maid. The setting of that sex scene, a storage room full of upset furniture, suggests an emotional disorder underlying the neat formality of eighteenth-century society. In this light, the film works as a domestic comedy about the anxieties in a sexual relationship, especially when the old Beethoven wonders why his proposed theater evening is not enough for the young Karl, and when Beethoven vituperates against the female gender.

But Morrissey rejects this reading:

It's inconceivable to think that Beethoven wanted sex with his nephew. That's a "liberal," Freudian idea. I never thought this. There was no eroticism. What he seemed to want was what Frankenstein and Dracuia wanted, control and possession. That's a much more powerful and confusing emotion. And although he never said it, maybe some kind of affection. His concerns with his nephew had more to do with his nephew's maturing, the reality that he was growing up and would no longer be under his control. I had his brother testify in court that Beethoven "tried to control his younger brothers." Wanting to control life makes him more sympathetic to me, a conservative, because remember, to me sex is the stupid religion of the "liberal." In none of my films has sex ever been anything that anybody ever "wanted." To read Beethoven's motives as sexual is to swallow the pervasive liberal lie that sex is not just a positive value but the entire meaning of life on the planet! When you believe that lie, naturally it follows that all behavior gravitates towards that goal.

Still, some sexual jealousy may be inferred – along with the rivalry for control – from Beethoven's horror of Karl being with and touching his own mother. Morrissey introduces this tension in the first meeting between mother and son as if it were a romantic tryst. Both the frigid setting at the ice pond and the characters' furtiveness suggest a romantic, not filial, meeting. The series of close-ups suggest that Karl resents the presence of his mother's lover, Michael (Walter Schupfer), as much as that of the uncle. Later, Karl fails to ask the court to transfer his custody to his mother because he is alienated by her having a lover scarcely older than he is. In casting a stately English actress (Jane Birkin) as Karl's mother, Joanna, Morrissey gives the character a distinguishing accent (shared only by David Cameron as the Viennese judge who orders Beethoven to send Karl away to boarding school). This identification directs us against Beethoven's view that the woman is a whore (Beethoven continually characterized women as "diseased whores"). So does her explanation of her economic and emotional dependence upon her callow lover. As if to heighten the sexual tension, Morrissey invented a key iconic character, Karl's mistress, Leonore.

Otherwise, Beethoven's history is so dramatic that no invention was needed. On the contrary, Morrissey toned down the fact that Karl's failed suicide attempt involved *two* guns fired through his head, because the image looked too comical. Beethoven, in his greed and vanity, charges people to stand outside his house to listen to his practicing and to watch him eat. He feeds his luncheon guests rotten eggs, which are dumped out upon his paying audience. In his paranoia, whether sexual or paternal, he spies constantly on Karl when the court orders him sent to a boarding school. Unfortunately, Beethoven does not see himself reflected in the history class he visits, on "Cicero: Dignity and Shame:...the decline of state authority into degeneracy and why this did happen." This exam subject summarizes once again Morrissey's critique of libertine democracy.

However, as with his other monsters, Morrissey allows Beethoven a scene of sympathy. "I was never your age, Karl. I was never young." Then Beethoven recounts his early thrust into responsibility to support his family when his alcoholic father could not, and his heartbreak when his one great love spurned him as "too ugly and too crazy." In another rare moment of self-awareness, Beethoven tells Karl about his own youthful adventures and his maddening syphilis. Morrissey included Beethoven's confession of profligacy to make it clear that his compulsions were not based on sexual

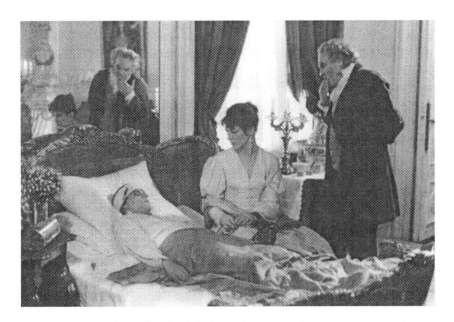

Beethoven's nephew after his failed suicide attempt (l. to r.): Dietmar Prinz, Jane Birkin, Wolfgang Reichmann.

attraction to his nephew. His disease is rather his horror of sexuality, which he shares with Morrissey's Frankenstein. But then, as Karl's actress advises (and as Morrissey has been telling us since *Flesh*), "Nobody loves anybody in just a normal way."

Perhaps the viewer's sympathy initially gravitates to the tortured nephew, deprived of his mother and childhood, forced against his will and nature into music studies, and hounded by his famous uncle's possessiveness even after his suicide attempt. In his most biting irony, Morrissey's closing title reports that Karl went through life bearing the burden of his uncle's name and the blame for his death.

But Morrissey says that he

> was always entirely sympathetic to Beethoven. I feel sorry for him because he was the victim of his own selfishness. I like the story because there's such a connection between his music and his life. I was struck by the fact that Beethoven never pontificated about his music. He'd say it was the best and then leave it at that. That was the one little area in which he was secure. Otherwise he was blind, helpless, a little like Mister Magoo. This makes him very human, even sympathetic.

In any case, Morrissey always tries to distribute his sympathy. "I don't have time to put someone I don't like, someone I'm not sympathetic to, in a movie," he says. "I never have any bad guys. I think in a comedy you tend to accept everyone. Everyone is sympathetic. I don't even have any villains in *Spike*." To keep a sympathetic balance, Morrissey had the nephew, Dietmar Prinz, suppress his smile and charm, so his severity would temper his appeal. Also, he never shows the nephew treat his uncle disrespectfully, until he leaves him to die.

In perhaps the most complex scene, Beethoven is maddened when Karl brings his actress to the premiere performance of Beethoven's Ninth. In his madness, deafness, and uncontrolled will, Beethoven proves unable to conduct the performance himself. Beethoven's historical deafness serves Morrissey as an emblem of the egotist locked in his private world, insensitive to the outside reality and to others' needs. After he carries on, deafly conducting the stopped musicians (which historically happened at a performance of his *Fidelio*), Beethoven is led away humiliated. But his music without him wins a triumphant recall. The scene dramatizes the gap between the man and his art, between artistic genius and humanity on the one hand and the cruelty and futility of a compulsive passion, on the other.

When the camera pans up a richly ornamented palace wall, Morrissey suggests that Beethoven's music may rise to the heavens and similarly inspire elevating emotions in its audience. But the character stays lumpily based in his own bitterness. Beethoven's music "speaks for what his life can't say, for what he was unable to do in his life, which was be nice to somebody."[23] Through one of its progenitors, Morrissey condemns the untrammeled will that romanticism celebrates – though he sympathizes with both of its victims, the object Karl and the subject Beethoven.

In response to his uncle's self-indulgence, Karl can only muster a more trivial version of the same. "Why can't you let me do it my way?" Karl reasonably asks, but his uncle has the rage of a publicly betrayed lover. So the great romanticism evokes a shallower one. In his adolescence, Karl can only rebel in the trivial snatch for sexual liberties. At the court hearing he lacks the will to escape his uncle's tyranny into his mother's less comfortable care. In a parallel declension of liberty, the actress offers Karl the alternative of sexual pragmatism: "It's a kind of love. It may not be forever. But there are people who understand these things. Not like your uncle." The kept woman's rationalization of her self-indulgence enhances the dignity of Beethoven's passion.

This character tension gives the film its contemporary relevance. Morrissey sees Beethoven as a very contemporary kind of character. He was very selfish, and had absolutely no regard for other people, which was unusual for the period, when everybody was so polite and well behaved.... I'm basically always telling the same story – how if you give people whatever they want, whether it's sex, drugs or dead bodies – or like Beethoven, you just do whatever you want – their lives are going to be empty and miserable. It's a comical subject, though, because you see the foolishness of it.[24]

Yet Karl is modern man in equally negative ways: shallow, unfeeling, and unimaginative. He can respond with only petulance to his uncle's genuinely felt emotion. In the balance between them Morrissey anatomizes the disintegration of our culture from codes of human responsibility to shallow self-interest. As Helen Knode saw it,

Slowly, your allegiance slides over to Beethoven, not because he gets nicer or saner – he doesn't – but because, in the midst of everything, he really does love and need his nephew. Reichmann's performance (one of the best of 1986 *or* 1988), combined with the seductive power of the music (notably the Ninth Symphony), places all the movie's weight on the side of "true feeling," however violently that true feeling expresses itself.[25]

Through the course of these three period films Morrissey deals with increasing explicitness with the master–servant relationship as an arena for psychological dominance. In all three, the master–servant relationship is bickering and tense, with the dominated servant chafing under a master's life-sucking tyranny, and the junior subverting the senior's stabilizing discipline. Meanwhile, the superior wastes from his own power and single-mindedness. Where Anton serves Dracula's mortal bloodlust, the savior is the lusty peasant wielding a liberating (read: enslaving) sexuality. The same actor/figure proves helpless in the Frankenstein world, where the children and servant Otto extend the mad scientist's craving for an unnaturally free sexuality. In Karl's revolt against Beethoven, sexual freedom is both the objective and the means of the shallow young man's independence.

In all three films, romantic heroes of remote time and place enact the source of modern self-indulgence and the lack of a moral foundation. The common curse of Frankenstein, Dracula, and Beethoven is their reductive liberty. "To a sex-worshipping liberal," Morrissey concludes, "all normal relations mean sexual relations. But the emotional urges towards family

94

and to control life and, in doing so, frustrate death, are far more complicated and more interesting and more dominant than the biological sex urge." His three monster heroes try to defeat death by controlling or arranging life. But they are thwarted by the unbridled sexuality of the young people they try to control. "Sex destroys the possibility of order and harmony and – in Beethoven's case especially – love and affection. To me, sexuality, never a desirable commodity to the main characters in my stories, was instead something to be against, something destructive. In my contemporary stories, it is always the last resort of the bored, of the empty, the desperate victims of the liberal tyranny." But his costume films revive larger spirits who sought to transcend sexual indulgence to place their stamp on a heroic future.

In all three cases, too, the female characters hold out a hope of regeneration or refuge. But as they are reduced to sexual diversion they lose their more humanizing effect. All three monsters are male, ravenous in appetite and ego and disdainful of any emotional life their women might otherwise kindle. Consequently, the three costume films are also family portraits. The families, however, live in artificial, self-imposed systems that prove morally insane in failing to sustain traditional standards. Frankenstein turns his back on even his irregular "family" to create an unnatural one. Dracula would suck the lifeblood out of the future of an old Italian family, which in its degeneracy has already sapped itself of vitality and worth. Beethoven destroys every corner of his own family to create his own household of the absurd. Morrissey's characters crave a familial union, but their only impulse is toward a sexual one. They are, as a result, doomed to their pathetic liberties.

5
The Street Life

After his comic horrors, Morrissey made three films about the realistic horror of the New York drug scene, but his theme remained the same: the waste of lives in self-indulgence. Echoing the hopeless world of *Trash*, the German drug dealer in *Mixed Blood* tells his mistress, "First we go down to the garbage." *Forty-Deuce* and *Mixed Blood* provide bleak insights into the despair and alienation of the drug culture. *Spike of Bensonhurst* balances this chaos with the blessed order – of the Mafia! The films are also unified by their fascination with language, especially the vituperation of the slum. What most unites the three films, however, is the theme of family. In all three the characters crave a family but are seduced by false "family" figures. For Morrissey the family represents traditional values, moral discipline, and guidance, all of which have been dissipated in destructive freedoms.

Forty-Deuce (1982)

Morrissey's first street-teen film is an inventive adaptation of Alan Bowne's chamber play about adolescents selling dope and sex in (as the title suggests) the 42nd Street hub of New York City. Morrissey preserved the play's unsentimental exposure of the exploitation of innocence and the rolling beauty of its profane dialogue. Though based on someone else's material, *Forty-Deuce* is pure Morrissey as it careens between shock and hilarity, vulgarity and tenderness, and presents his most characteristic theme. Its characters' liberty enslaves them both to their own arbitrary impulses and to exploitation by others. To Morrissey, it exposes "the great liberal lie of the last thirty to forty years: Do whatever you want."

A twelve-year-old runaway boy dies in a hotel bed of an overdose. Ricky (Kevin Bacon)[1] and Blow (Mark Keyloun), two male prostitutes, try to frame

96

a rich customer, Mr. Roper (Orson Bean). For most of the film, Ricky and Blow disdain the voluble authority of their pimp, Augie (Harris Laskowy). But when their plot fails, their illusions of independence collapse. Ricky kills himself in the toilet and Blow resigns himself to working for Augie's unseen boss, Mike. Some black dealers are framed to take the rap in Roper's stead, but the boys seem equally doomed.

The original play establishes metaphors of self-delusion, exploitation, and hypocrisy in the characters' exchanges around the new boy's corpse. Augie's teenage sex market is presented as a bleak microcosm of normal capitalism: "I lose my protection you bitches have to suck it off in the street. Mike blacklist you every hotel in the Square. This here is clean, it's quick, and it's guaranteed. [pause] This here is like a Burger King." Or as Mr. Roper tells Blow, "I derive the most intense pleasure from knowing that your body is being purchased in the same way as toothpaste or a pair of shoes. It's tit for tat, kids. Our tyranny as opposed to yours." The play encapsulates Morrissey's view of modern man turned into a commodity. Augie's favorite nickname for the boys is "testicle," reducing them to their salable part. Blow summarizes his "liberated" existence with Beckettian simplicity: "I sell dick, I sell dope. I come, I go."

But the play's "central metaphor, which was the basis of the play, that made me want to bring it to the screen," says Morrissey, was its presentation of modern life as a toilet. "I had never encountered any play or film that could even remotely be considered as antisex, and here was this astonishing indictment of the liberal horror. Of course, the play was a failure in the eyes of the liberal reviewing establishment. But no one identified what it so obviously was, an equation of sex to the toilet." The reiterated phrase "fuckin' toilet" is not just an oath but an equation.

Morrissey amplifies the theme. Augie is sent to look for Ricky in the bus terminal toilet, "the one at the top of the stairs, for the Jersey commuters. He likes that one. It's like his head office. He's asleep there, asleep on the toilet." This disclosure jars even the hardened Augie: "Asleep on the fuckin' toilet!?!" Augie finds him there. As he slaps him into (relative) consciousness, Augie yells about the dead child in the hotel room.

In Morrissey's chilling addition, a well-dressed commuter (Rudy de Bellis) witnesses the scene and continues about his ablutions, fussing with his hair and lingering unfazed, his only interest apparently being to attract Ricky. As this bathroom drama continues, Augie goes off-frame to urinate and Ricky vomits in the sink. The stranger takes the opportunity to make a sexual pass at Ricky. This courtship continues when the stranger defecates in the neighboring stall. In this scene, Morrissey presents the world of liberal

The hotel room set in *Forty-Deuce*: Kevin Bacon, Mark Keyloun.

license in terms of vomiting, defecation, urinating, commercial sex, and an overall atmosphere of social nonconcern.

In the same vein, Ricky always goes into the hotel toilet to shoot up. He dies as he lived, on the toilet. In the last line of the play, Crank rehearses Mitchell's alibi, namely that they last saw Ricky "asleep on the fuckin' toilet." In Morrissey's metaphor, the toilet is not just the sordid summary of liberal sexual license but a site of nonconsciousness. "To buy the liberal lie is, to me, to live and die in and on a toilet." In the consistency of Morrissey's moral vision throughout his film career, the metaphor is as logical as scatological.

Morrissey kept almost all of the cast of the play's second stage production.[2] In the only change, Essai Morales, just out of the High School of the Performing Arts and before doing *Bad Boys*, provided a Puerto Rican version of the Jewish character Mitchell, but without replacing the schtick. The effect of a Puerto Rican doing Yiddish inflections is to suggest a fertile ethnic community — that does not, however, diminish the characters' alienation.

In order to convey the claustrophobic, *Huis Clos* hell of the hotel room, Morrissey used the stage set and planned to film it in one day, in continuous takes on two cameras. Instead, he went with a union cast and shot the performance in five days. He shot the first forty-five minutes with a hand-held 35 mm camera in four days. In contrast to the long, free scenes in the first half, Morrissey filmed the last half of the play, as the action plunges to its conclusion, in real time. This breakneck forty-five-minute climax was shot with two adjacent 16 mm cameras in two equal takes. The fade-out halfway through to reload the cameras reminds us of the work's theatricality. From this directness the audience feels trapped and propelled through the characters' inevitable disintegration. There are no escapes or comforting cinematic devices (such as music) to alleviate the sordidness of the characters' lives. "It's appropriate to the idea that people are trapped in the toilet of license and they can't get out," says Morrissey. "People squirm and want to get out of the theater but they can't. Like the debris in a flushed toilet, it can't escape its downward spiral." As if to imply complicity in the audience's helpless presence, Morrissey early in the film shows the new street kid in bed, under a green blanket, as he stirs, tries to rise, then falls back dead. Where the play opened on the corpse, Morrissey makes us witness the dying. The runaway child acts out the last gasps of our innocence.

The strategy of the long take also serves the strange beauty of the characters' cascading speeches, oratorical in their rhythm and energy. The street language is often racist, as in Ricky's tirade against the Greeks: "Fuckin' Greeks eighty-five cents for Diet-Rite four dollars for a lousy pancake. Fuckin' Greeks fuckin' mothers. They come over here make a few bucks offa hot cigarettes souvlaki sandwiches. Buy up every shit corner this town."

The language is also, obviously, obscene. But Morrissey's view is warmly multicultural. The most aggressive in a line of young hustlers is a Japanese (Yukio Yamamoto) reciting his wares: "Coke – speed – cock. Coke – speed – cock." The characters are not so egalitarian. Here Mitchell summarizes his father's concern:

> My ka-fucking dad. I wear these hot pants once for the big fag crusade up Christopher every year? Pink hot pants ride up my thighs you could see my balls. Said I jiggled like the fringe on a chenille bedspread. You think he give a shit? All the time tanked to the tits, he just hope I ain't giving no blow jobs to no *shvartzers*? Didn't want his kid goin' down on no *shvartzers*. Only the *goyim,* he says. He says, all that pink skin and clean hair how could they give you disease? My dad.

Strikingly, this is the only real family relationship in the work. Yet it is both absent and negligent. Though the speech is shot around a pool table, it lacks the manly camaraderie of either family or play. To Morrissey, "The kids are my most demented family unit yet. With Augie the father figure and Mike even bigger, the invented society is far crueler than anything the Inquisition could ever have dreamed of being."

Against the verbal violence, Morrissey posits the occasional gesture of unexpected tenderness, such as Blow's fondling of the dead boy's hair and his dedication to preserving the corpse from harm or even exposure. The latter nicety is abandoned in the film's last action. The sheet is brusquely whipped off the corpse, a chilling reminder of Blow's failure on every front. Blow even buys the runaway a "tacky" T-shirt, saying, "I got it small cause you're so fuckin' little." The tender gift turns violent when Roper whips the dead boy with it, angry at his (understandable) unresponsiveness. Morrissey suggests Blow's own fragility in a close-up of him tapping the glass windows, as he exults in being an independent hustler (i.e., not yet in the power of a pimp). These tender gestures suggest a need for human connection that is narrowed into the only emotion the characters recognize, the sexual.

Here Crank summarizes his knowledge: "Most girls spring for the titties. But for the pussies? Ya gotta have big bucks for the pussies. This I know." Though the subject seems to be heterosexual prostitution, Crank is actually discussing the cost of sex change operations. So topsy-turvy is this libertine chaos that "girls" in the play always means "boys," as "freedom" in this context means "enslavement," and "knowledge" is "ignorance." Hence Blow's equation: "I know Roper. I do Roper." The characters' only knowledge is carnal.

So, too, Roper's "power" is his "weakness." With only the corpse to hear him, Roper keeps up his pretenses. He first pretends lack of interest in the "sleeping" boy, then says that he desires only theater, role-playing. But he finally cuddles up to the corpse with a confession: "I'm so cold. Please. Don't think badly of me, I just want . . . Please." The powerful but pathetic businessman seeks warmth from a stone-cold corpse. To Morrissey, here as for Frankenstein and Dracula, "Touching people is a kind of death. That one moment of affection, of touch, is the indication that sex, that any kind of touching itself is death." Confronted with the death and exposure, the respectable Roper hides under the bed until he is absolved by his dependable menial, Augie. With Augie's boss, Mike, and Mitchell's father, both authority figures, unseen, Morrissey shows the squalor of a world without social order or self-restraint.

Not limited to the play's single set, Morrissey punctuates the first half with silent aerial (God's-eye?) views of the cityscape dwarfing the characters.

These shots confirm the narrowness of the boys' lives, even in the wide outside world. Hence the comedy of Crank confusedly getting directions to Queens. Morrissey frames the commodified boys ("We sell tickets to our insides") against the macho glamour of the subway ads for a Burt Reynolds movie and Marlboro cigarettes. A cinema marquee over Mitchell promises *Sex Tool* and *Wrangler in Jeans*. Ricky obscures a poster for Harvey Fierstein's *Torch Song Trilogy;* beside Morrissey's violent world Fierstein's gay order pales.[3]

Morrissey's first climax occurs when Ricky and Blow strike a dangerous deal with two blacks. "We're all niggers, nigger," the black woman tells the white Blow, forging (in both senses) a fraternity of victims while she protects her territory. When Ricky acts to meet his debts to Mike and to the blacks and at the same time to dispose of the corpse, Morrissey suddenly introduces a wide-screen skyline shot, then plays out the rest of the film in a screen split into two equal squares of action. The sudden widening of the rooftop image brings an exhilaration and scope, quickly dashed by the characters' fates.

This device sets off the climax more complexly than the split screen in *Dionysus '69* (1970) or the double screen in *The Chelsea Girls*.[4] For example, Jonathan Rosenbaum finds that this "variable binocular effect" approximates "a vision that sees the whole world through a veil of cross-eyed and two-faced duplicity – a context where every act has at least two motives and hence potential cross-purposes, and every event becomes at once a moment of moral horror and an act of aesthetic perception."[5]

Morrissey's split screen also establishes a metaphor for the boys' situation. They are together yet isolated, in separate boxes of desperation. In this sense the split screen seems set up by the toilet scene, in which the commuter is attracted to Ricky but oblivious to what Ricky and Augie say and do. Later, at a coffee shop counter, Ricky and Blow talk openly about the dead boy and their "deal with some fuckin' niggers," oblivious to the two men beside them, one black. These lives are as isolated from each other within the same frame as they are when the screen shows two frames together. The doubled screen literalizes the characters' isolation.

The effects are manifold. By filming one side slightly closer than the other, Morrissey conveys the boys' self-detachment, suggesting both their alienation and their drugged stupor. The doubled action coheres with the heroes' compulsive nervous energy, which is also expressed in their constant chatter and activity. The wider screen seems needed now to contain the characters and their exploding drama. Conversely, its duplication of image reiterates the narrowness of the boys' world. Roper explodes over both screens for his tirade against Ricky and Blow. With the double screen Morrissey avoids cutting away from his actors and their compelling characters.

So rich are the inflections that Morrissey seems to have choreographed the flow of characters and camera through and between the separate images. From high on the right screen, Roper tells Ricky and Blow (who are isolated on the left one): "Speaking of you as 'product' is our way of keeping you boys at arm's length." Then the screens (like the characters) are briefly bridged by a close-up on a joint that Blow hands Roper across the division. The joint crosses the "arm's length" gap between the mutual exploiters. Their connection is a stoned illusion.

Ricky seems to have fallen between the screens when Roper and Blow discuss the kid's daylong drug binge. When Roper finally cuddles up with the corpse, the right screen shows a close-up of his hand, holding him. That is to say, the man's embrace of the corpse is seen in two registers: the detached long shot and the intimate point of grip. Given the implications of the scene, the emotional effect is complex. The long shot presents the paradox of the man hugging a corpse for warmth. The close-up, emphasizing the urgency of the grip, makes the death seem irrelevant. After the fade-out, the action resumes with the hand close-up on the left, implying a passage of time and some action, with Ricky, then Blow, entering on the right screen. The right screen assumes the shifting weight of power. Augie commands it when he tells Blow that he (Blow) now belongs to Mike.

The doubled action often serves as a Brechtian underlining to the politics of the scene. For one thing, the viewer is forced out of passivity, forced to choose on which screen to focus, whether to watch the speaker or the listener. As this encourages political analysis, Mr. Roper stands for the adult crust of "legitimate" moral and economic power that abuses and exploits the boys, for all their delusions of freedom. Though his power seems at first economic, after he crumbles he derives his power from the social hierarchy that simply prefers his class over the boys or the blacks. So a political dimension is added to Blow's earlier description of his "straight" clients who live normal, respectable, middle-class heterosexual lives, who loudly disdain queers, yet can themselves find sexual gratification only in a bought homosexual encounter. To end the film Morrissey pans – against the normal rightward sweep of the eye – across the dark black right square to the cold white corpse on the left. This eloquent close-up literalizes the various characters' death-in-life.

Despite the film's harrowing subject matter and uncompromising language, it is consistent with Morrissey's inclination toward moral comedy.

"Most people reviewing the films would say there was no judgment made," Morrissey says, "But that they were comedies is a kind of judgment on the subject. Showing the foolishness of people's lives, which is the basis of comedy, is in effect a kind of moral judgment."[6]

Mixed Blood (1984)

After the theatrical *Forty-Deuce*, Morrissey hit the streets with a drama about drug-gang wars in Alphabet City (Avenues A, B, C, and D in the Lower East Side of New York). In the opening shot, the foreground presents the shells of burned-out tenements; like a misty phantom, behind stands the Empire State Building. As this ghost of materialist aspiration wafts in the background, the camera pans down to the livelier life signs of murals and graffiti. The film lies implicit in that shot. Morrissey defines capitalist America in terms of the lawless subculture of drugs and prostitution – and the sacrifice of the young. His "quote" of the Empire State Building inevitably evokes Warhol's eight-hour meditation, *Empire* (1964), which has been called the longest establishing shot in film history.[7] But where Warhol subordinated his theme – the emptiness of American materialism and imperialism – to the numbing challenge of "seeing" (that is, enduring) the legendary bore, Morrissey's engaging fiction, with bright colors and the music of life, reduces the building to a background specter.

A flamboyant Brazilian woman, Rita La Punta – "Not La Puta!" – (Marilla Pera), and her vulpine but slow son Thiago (Richard Ulacia) run the Maceteros (Butchers), a gang of underage boys, young enough that they can kill without going to jail. In this world there is no childhood. The playground is used to recruit new gang members.[8] The young gang members enter the film by climbing through a hole in the wall, like rats from an abandoned building. For drug turf they battle the Master Dancers, an older gang led by Juan the Bullet (Angel David). Rita calls him "spic scum," believing in the Portuguese's superiority over the Hispanics. The Maceteros become vulnerable when Thiago is led astray by an uptown blonde, Carol (Linda Kerridge). In another example of the intriguing inconsistency of Morrissey's characters, Rita brings the blonde to her son, then rages at their relationship. "I like complicating a character," says Morrissey. "If you make them embody contrary thinking then they're a little bit funny, a little more human." Rita's attempt to betray Carol leads to her own and Thiago's capture.

The film ends on Thiago, tears clouding his eyes, his back turned against his mother. She reiterates her demand that "you must always do what your

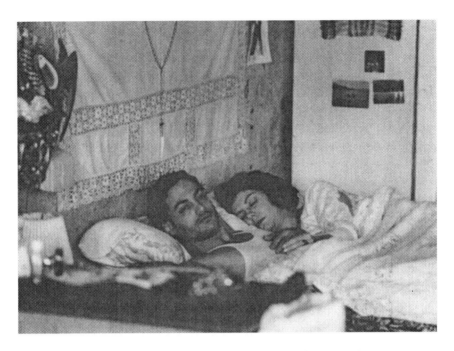

The last scene of *Mixed Blood*: a pensive Thiago wonders about his mother's loyalty.

mother tells you, you hear? Always." But Thiago seems doomed to wonder if his mother betrayed him too. The film's closest relationship has been forever undermined. If the film's dominant image is the city ruins, its dominant theme is their analogue, the ruined heart of human relationship, most touchingly seen between the stunted son and his powerful mother.

By dint of her energy and colorful language, Rita grabs and holds the audience's sympathy. In some ways she's like her own heroine, Carmen Miranda, saying, "She was the Abraham Lincoln of Brazil. And she knew it." In a buoyant interlude, Rita does a vigorous version of "Tico Tico" at her grandson's christening. The scene establishes Rita's exuberance and the strength she draws from her cultural tradition. Singing, she weaves through the room, circling back to Thiago, but drawing together everyone at her celebration. Her music expands her "family." She is the group's unifying, even harmonizing spirit. But these values are interrupted when the enemy gang sweeps in and murders Rita's son-in-law and several of her boys.

The attack represents the chaos in the openness that drew Rita to America. Rita fled Brazil because she saw America as the promised land of unbridled capitalism. She finds it safer to deal in drugs in America because there are no laws: "No. Nothing." The bleeding-heart society lets off underage killers. The cops are all sensitive, flexible, understanding folks, that is, "bought." They are so harmless that a teenage drug dealer safely calls one a nigger dyke. The only real threat is the outsider, a German drug supplier (Ulrich Berr), who disturbs the "order" by not treating his client gangs equitably and by introducing the fatal Carol into Rita's "family." Rita thrives from the moral debility of the liberal culture. Her gang buys new recruits from a community theater group that is publicly funded to provide kids with alternatives to the gang life.

As suggested in Rita's harmonizing dance, family is an important theme in *Mixed Blood*. Though Thiago is Rita's only son, she considers all the boys in her gang to be her children. She orders them to avoid drugs and to change into clean underwear before going out to kill. "I run a clean house," she insists of her dilapidated domain. When she orders one boy to take out the garbage – "Do it now or no television" – she seems to be living a fun house mirror *Leave it to Beaver*. She is as generous in buying a funeral for her "almost fourteen" hench-kid thrown off a roof as she is for her first grandchild's christening. "I loved Bobby. He was a little bit stupid. But all of you are – a little bit – stupid."

Morrissey's point is that Rita's "family" is a false community. It is ersatz, manufactured in the absence of a value-centered genuine family. Her sentiments gloss her greed and vanity. In a similar vein, her jealousy of Carol proves an unmotherly possessiveness, not unrelated to the fact that Rita sleeps with her son Thiago, even if we don't see them have sex. Rita prefers to have Thiago sleep with his Toni (Geraldine Smith), whom he also deploys as a prostitute, than with the "bitch with white hair and white face and white lips," Carol, who is a greater threat to Rita's hold on him. Rita's interest in Thiago's sexuality parallels Beethoven's in his nephew's; the issue is control. For Morrissey, "Maybe she has too much power and gets mixed up in her attempts to control her son's life, but for me she means well. At least she's not looking for sex herself, although she tolerates it among her subordinates. I'm not against power or control coming from someone who represents a real family, such as a mother over her sons. What I don't like is power coming from commissars and liberal ideologies."

One scene makes the theme of family explicit. Just before the climactic shoot-out, Hector (Marcelino Rivera) asserts the moral and emotional superiority of his having a real family over a parallel false family, Juan the Bullet's gang. While both men strut and posture, on a ruined old car behind them two young children sit in a warm embrace, perhaps the film's most touching – if not indeed only – image of selfless and caring responsibility. One swarthy, the other blonde, they suggest the doomed image of sentiment for which the larger action allows no hope. For his part, Hector is like Rita in having a past (as a former policeman) to support his present identity and a family alternative to his criminal definition. Earlier he was eager to leave a meeting with underworld forces in order to get to his son's confirmation. But Hector remains negative because his "family" aspect is too peripheral to his life. Despite its selfish use, Rita's "family" does include warmth and values. In the moral vacuum of her society there is no alternative care. As well as power there is – in Morrissey's view – maternal care in Rita's order that Thiago "always do what your mother says."

In the same spirit, the film's title (changed from the planned *Alphabet City*) refers to the ethnic mix of the modern ghettoes. The drug market is, to them, a tug-of-war between niggers, chinks, and spics. As Rita insists on purity, she refuses to use blacks to do her killing unless they're also Hispanic: "Never mix blood," she says. In a comic counterpoint, the Jewish caterer plans for the Brazilian christening a mix of burritos, chopped liver, pastrami, Brazilian beer, and a Cookie Monster ice cream cake: the American melting pot as menu. As Morrissey told John Kobal, the melting pot reference of the title puts the film in the tradition of immigrants' problems in the United States, but they now face the additional problem of, as Morrissey puts it, "too much freedom! Total laissez-faire towards everything."[9]

The gangs' various rites betray the violence and alienation within their ostensible family spirit. Carol is barely spared a humiliating initiation when she becomes Thiago's woman. The Master Dancers ritually beat Stingray (Fabio Urena) and carve an X into his stomach when he seeks to leave the gang; they beat Comanche (Pedro Sanchez) when he joins. On both boys there is family pressure. Stingray leaves the gang because his entire biological family has vowed not to speak to him until he does. That is, he recovers proper values when he accepts discipline from his real family, which has real concern for him. The genuine family is scorned by the false family, as Juan the Bullet scorns Hector's. In contrast, Comanche follows his crippled brother into the Master Dancers in order to kill Thiago, who shot the brother. As it happens, Comanche also suffers a cigarette-butt initiation from Thiago. He could have won sufficient access without first joining the rival Master Dancers family. But Comanche prefers to be an undercover member of the enemy gang. He seems to need the gang-family motive and secret cover to validate, not to expedite, his real-family revenge. The gangs provide a false-family alternative to the traditional family's values and community.

That is one of the points of the comic scene in which Juan the Bullet lectures one of his goons on cleanliness and urination. As the scene occurs just before the gang shoots up Rita's celebration, two "family" episodes are paralleled. In Morrissey's obligatory liberal toilet, one goon washes his hands before urinating. Juan, in a false-fatherly way, tells him to wash afterward instead. In a harsh-father twist, Juan then holds his knife to the goon's throat for arguing the right to wash and piss as one wishes. The scene is comic, but it establishes the tyranny of the gang leadership (the false father), the need for ritual order both to the individual and in the family/gang, and the contrary need (that may draw boys into gangs) to find ways to be nonconformist. His concern for his charges' cleanliness makes Juan parallel Rita ("Suppose they took you to prison with that dirty underwear?"). This comic interlude, like Rita's "Tico Tico," helps to set off a violent murder. Both "families" establish trivial and debasing social orders in the vacuum of a valueless society.

The setting of Rita's and Carol's later capture establishes a wider commercial context for the metaphor of Rita's family. It happens in what Rita calls a "bubblegum rock and roll store for the spics," a store that specializes in Menudo paraphernalia. Menudo is the popular but synthetic young group whose members are expelled from the singing – that is, commercial – "family" when they grow too old for the teenyboppers. Rita is aware of their parallel, as both exploit sentiment and sell (out) youth. She rejects a "Johnny" T-shirt because he represents "Old Menudo." She reminisces warmly about Miguel, who once came to that store with (of course) his mother: "They lost Miguel. They lose many boys. Like me." Of course, that "lose" is an evasive euphemism for "mortally exploit." Like her, Menudo commercially exploits children. More generally, the drug and music scenes become an emblem of America's commodification of life and values, a symptom of capitalism.

Though Morrissey casts a cold eye on the "family" betrayals and the slaughter of young boys, he is fascinated by the life he records. With anthropological respect, he details the strategies by which drugs are dealt in the city and to its human ruins. His unemphatic long shots, which seem to record action inadvertently discovered, propose a documentary view with no moral point to push. One long shot records the fluttering departure, then the quick return, of the flock of drug addicts lining up for their fix. The orderly return suggests that in even this chaos lurks a recidivist need for order.

Morrissey's subtlety in this film can be seen in his use of José (Rodney Harvey), the baby-faced boy who seems to be Thiago's closest aide. Behind

The "family" in *Mixed Blood*: Thiago (Richard Ulacia), Rita (Marilla Pera), and José (Rodney Harvey).

the opening credits the boy appears with the older Toni and Thiago. The trio recalls the "family" formed by James Dean, Natalie Wood, and Sal Mineo before the ending of *Rebel Without a Cause*. (Change "Rebel" to "Rubble" and you have *Mixed Blood*.) José's youthfulness makes a possible "couple" out of Thiago and Toni before we know anything else about them. Of course, Thiago then sells Toni as a prostitute, who (by their dialogue of glances) services her johns out of dedication to him. Something of Rita's possessiveness, Thiago's stunted development, and the pathology of the family structures can be inferred from the later trio scenes. Rita supplants Toni in the walk with Thiago and José. Later Carol takes Thiago out of his safe territory. José's attendance redefines both couples as a parody family. Without the boy, the image would be of two people, whether alone or in a couple. He makes them seem to be a family, but only "seem." In all three cases José also helps establish the power struggle between the three women. When Carol tells Rita she's not really interested in Thiago, Morrissey includes a reaction shot of José, witness to Thiago's shifting romantic field.

He also seems to be special to Rita, for she will not let him kill anyone. He carries the gun for Thiago. One inference from her protection of José is that even Rita's own son may prove expendable.

At the same time, José expresses an extremely limited understanding and an unbridled will. Despite the undertaker's assertion that no green flowers exist, José insists he "Get them!" for his (inevitably imminent) funeral. Perhaps José seems so precious because he's an image of the beautiful youth doomed. In a bleaker comic register, what strikes José as "fuckin' sick" is not Juan the Bullet's threat to cut out Rita's pussy and send it to Thiago by Federal Express, but that the shoot-out should have happened at Menudo's! As no one remarks on José's limited vision, his puerile understanding fairly represents his world.

For all the film's subtleties, however, its characteristic effects are dramatic. It encountered censorship problems for its explicit scenes of drug use, though at least one character is shown to die for being "stuck on" the needle, a weakness that enabled Rita (literally) to go for the jugular. In Ontario the film was banned for several years, although articulate protest won the film a single screening at the Toronto Film Festival and limited screenings later.

More upsetting still is the gore in the murder scenes. The young thugs and Carol are killed with visible splattering of blood. The violence jars all the more against the film's detached tone. At the same time, Morrissey's deadpan humor has a distancing effect. Thus Carol asks for some gum just before she is killed; after her brains have been shot out she remarks, "Jeez, I must look like hell." This brief life after death fits a film about such deathlike lives, which operate free of the brain anyway.

But Morrissey does not sensationalize his material. He needs the shock to dramatize the cost of remaining cool about the anomie he has discovered in the meaner streets. His unflinching view of the gangs' initiation torture – the slashed stomach of the leaver, the cigarettes butted on the enterer – are a necessary repellent from the appeal of gang membership. They also suggest the irrational appeal gang membership must have to its initiates. Morrissey's bloodletting is shocking so that we can't enjoy the comfort of Hollywood's more conventional killing scenes, where "discretion" glamorizes murder. The last murder in the film is handled that bloodless way – we hear a shot, then the German slides cleanly down out of the frame – as if to remind us how assuring are more decorous deaths.

In *Mixed Blood* Morrissey plays comedy and horror against each other, but the horror and gore predominate. When he returned to the street life for *Spike of Bensonhurst*, he shifted the balance toward the comic. The result was a sunnier, more commercial film, whose unsettling effects were verbal and ethical rather than the visceral disturbances felt from *Mixed Blood*.

Spike of Bensonhurst (1988)

The title may suggest a rough misfit's experience in a prep school. But this prep school, Bensonhurst, is a tough Italian neighborhood in New York where, as it happens, race riots erupted in 1989. The street-smart hero learns the social graces and manners appropriate to his aspirations. The film's title in its planning stages was *Throwback*. "That's a 'throwback' to the past," says Morrissey. "He was obviously a new kind of hero for me." Morrissey rewrote the character, toning down the immorality and meanness of the first draft, written by *Forty-Deuce* playwright Alan Bowne. The loudmouthed, undisciplined, vain, corrupt, conning loser finally finds his niche – as a cop. The agent of his reform is that mainstay of American values and social order, the Mafia! This film exemplifies Morrissey's Conservatism of the Absurd.

When Morrissey probes an irregular, even grotesque, society, he uncovers the conventions and strictures of a John O'Hara novel. As in *Mixed Blood* there is an ethnographic element in his gangs' dance, in their patois and in the ethnic ceremonies, whether a bar mitzvah, the goons' interview with Spike's mother, or the mafioso's party in honor of Spike's released convict father. Though the line dance derives from *Saturday Night Fever*, Spike uses it as a hook on an Italian blonde: "This music is, like, your heritage, hundreds of years old." As usual, Morrissey's record of neighborhood ways conveys man's need to subordinate his individualism to the collective good: "Better a double standard than no standards at all," he says.

Spike Fumo (Sasha Mitchell) is a handsome young Italian boxer who hopes to work his way up in the system, first by throwing his fights, then by marrying Angel (Maria Patillo), the pampered coed daughter of the local Mafia boss, Baldo Cacetti (Ernest Borgnine). As his sidekick (Rodney Harvey again) describes him in Morrissey's upside-down world, "He's been to reform school. He's a dropout. Very ambitious." Spike's father, Pete, is in jail, taking the rap for Cacetti, who had to "rough up" some "hookers" that turned out to be cops in drag. His sacrifice keeps the Fumo family in the "Family's" good books, with a monthly check from the local mafioso. The combination of liberal welfare check and gangland stipend typifies Morrissey's pragmatic family. It also recalls Holly's pathetic faith in welfare as an emblem of respectability in *Trash*. But Cacetti wants a more stable son-in-law than Spike. When Spike is banished from Bensonhurst for persisting in seeing Angel, he moves into Red Hook to live with the family of a Puerto Rican boxer, Bandana (Rick Aviles). Here, Spike starts to live out a shriveled parody of *Rocky*. As he trains for his big fight he teaches the little boys who follow him the "Brooklyn alphabet" ("Fuckin' A, Fuckin' B....") and the social justice of organized crime. Spike asserts a superior morality by attacking the drug dealers who infest the schoolyard. He also impregnates India (Talisa Soto), his host's sister, without even pretending to have dropped his interest in Angel. Spike's attack on the drug trade embarrasses Cacetti, so he lifts his banishment and agrees to let Spike win a fight and marry Angel. But Cacetti reneges when he finds Spike asleep on the bed of Cacetti's young wife, Sylvia (Anne DeSalvo), after an innocent game of cards. He has Spike's father released early from jail. But at the celebration – and with Spike's parents' consent – Cacetti's goons smash Spike's hands. Angel marries her accountant suitor, the preppy Italian, Justin. At the end, Spike's fatherhood of Cacetti's grandson is acknowledged, but Spike is blunted, resignedly married to the Puerto Rican girl and secure in his position in the underworld establishment as a cop.

The film defines family values, but through a range of offbeat families. There are uneasy tensions between Cacetti and his stiletto-sharp second wife, and between her and her stepdaughter Angel. With her husband in jail, Spike's mother (Geraldine Smith) has a live-in lesbian lover of unconventional language: "How fuckin' dare you talk to your fuckin' mother like that?" Nor does Spike's mother speak to him like a Hallmark valentine: "Pussy. Asshole. Fuck," she says. She seems an older image of Spike, stealing her pleasures as he steals his. Spike especially steals food: steaks from two women and pizza from Justin.

The chilled Italian families contrast to the heat and proliferation of children in the Puerto Rican family. The matriarch (Antonia Rey) shows no concern about Spike's attraction to her vulnerable daughter. This relationship is conveyed in such fleeting nuances that we are surprised to learn it has happened. Angel encourages Spike to impregnate her as a way of forcing her father to return him to Bensonhurst. As Spike perfunctorily obliges her, we may well doubt his romantic commitment. In this context, India seems ennobled by the reticent treatment of her romance with Spike. When shown love scenes are so ludicrous those unshown retain the potential of romance. As in Dracula's union with Esmerelda, Morrissey's discretion in offscreen intimacy here is as radical as his graphic scenes were in the sixties.

The conclusion establishes a neat balance of new, restored, and extended families, a coherent social order. Spike's parents are reunited, Angel has an appropriate husband, Spike has an appropriate family and career, and over the entire society presides the old mafioso whose authority the upstart had challenged. By intercutting Spike's fight victory with Cacetti's fete for Spike's dad, Morrissey emphasizes Spike's alienation. He has left both his own and the Mafia family. His sole support is India, who selflessly advises him to take the ordered dive. When Spike finally takes his place in the Mafia "family," when he finally reins in his will, his family reaffirms the social order. The father–son tension is bathetically replayed on the television soap opera that disappoints Cacetti and his goons during Spike's visit. In the television show, a man has an affair with his son's wife (an age match that mirrors the assumed infidelity that aroused Cacetti's ire).

If the extended and warring family is one of Morrissey's most striking metaphors, its opposite is the boxing ring, ever the mirror of the larger society. The boxing announcer scrupulously details the fighters' lineage to help the fans identify with them. This sport has long served Hollywood as a symbolic arena for contrary drives in the American psyche: the need for social control and order versus the individualistic urge to take one's fate in hand and fight to success. The genre validates violence and unbridled ambition, but frames it away in the squared circle instead of in the home, office, or faculty lounge. To validate the fighter's violent hunger, that image of social regulation, the fight manager, is conventionally characterized as corrupt. Where the family represents the subordination of personal desires to communal ones, the ring is where the individual will is allowed legitimate unleashing. So the "family" exercises its control over Spike by fixing his fights. He self-destructs by refusing to lose: He loses by winning. In Morrissey's system, even this most individualist arena offers only an illusion of independence, for the rebel individual submits to his own destructive will. Cacetti can change the fix, but his fighter can't, least of all by winning. Morrissey reaffirms the collective good over the individual, against the conventions of the genre.

Spike's home boxing club, the Rome, is a small, dingy gym hardly evocative of its namesake. The discordant classicism recalls the Greek temple in *Madame Wang's*. The Puerto Rican equivalent is even more bathetic: "José's World Famous Gym of Puerto-Rican Boxing Champions and lawn furniture." Boxers are reduced to an ornamental commodity. All of the public fights are staged in tiny, constricted areas before small clutches of spectators. Though this world constricts its exuberant, thrusting egos, the arena pretends to importance.

Spike makes a metaphor out of his own name when he attributes his self-destructive impulses to parental neglect: "I always have to drive the spike in a little deeper," he says. Spike's ego makes him a wedge within existing orders: between his mother and her lover, between Cacetti and Angel, between Angel and her "squarehead" suitor, between the Red Hook drug dealers and the Puerto Rican community that accepts Spike, and ultimately between his ego and his real self-interest. Had Spike won in his own way he would be like Morrissey's Beethoven. Luckily for him, he is put in his place. So is Cacetti, who becomes sympathetic when he answers to higher social authority. Cacetti abandons Spike because he "went a little too far. He got no sense of proportion." Simply, Spike is the thick edge of a wedge. He is reaccepted when he submits to the various "family" roles assigned him, no longer embarrassing his (rather more embarrassing) parents, taking the job given him in the community, and playing along with his fatherhood of one son and his family life with the other.

Curiously, in *Mixed Blood* a cop observes that the estimable Rita La Punta's name means "the spike" in Portuguese. The characters' parallel goes further. Spike practices a nonsexual form of prostitution in his dive-taking career as a boxer and in his sexual use by the aggressive Angel. Like Rita, Spike tries to use his illegitimate son as his way of climbing up the criminal hierarchy.

In her admiration for what she views as the superior Italian society, India's mother (Antonia Rey) gives history lessons on the great Italian leaders: Julius Caesar, Mussolini, Al Capone. However suspect her heroes, she sustains her culture by teaching classes in a school washroom as the students sit outside the stalls. The surreal setting (based on an actual overcrowding in a Spanish class reported at a Brooklyn high school) coheres with Morrissey's recurring toilet imagery: "All the bourgeois values flushed down the toilet have to be reproduced even in the most obscene conditions," Morrissey says. "You can't live without them." But like an off-key Spartacus, Spike leads the kids out of the toilet into a deserted pastel swimming pool.

The matriarch is thrilled to host Spike, saying, "The dream of my life – a Mafia connection – to clear up this misery." That is, the character who alone preserves cultural self-respect and dignity is so committed to social authority that she values its last outpost, the illegal Mafia. She is so innocent that she's disappointed when Spike wins a fight straight; she'd hoped it was fixed like television wrestling. The joke is emblematic of the mad careening of a society lacking consistent values. So, too, Cacetti's wife advises her stockbroker to invest in high-fat foods, that emblem of self-indulgence: "They're the next craze. Trust me."

Morrissey parallels the film's two main mothers. Both are clear-sighted, aggressive women. Despite her insults, Spike's mother has a fair sense of his character and worth. She seems to be a projection of her son's future: a wild, unconventional spirit eventually brought to toe the family line. But until her husband returns from jail to control her, she proves as self-indulgent as her son (who also inherited her Irish looks). In contrast, the Puerto Rican mother has a solid ethical core, a sense of historical context (however comical), and independence. She explains why she named her daughter India: "I wanted to name her Gandhi, but it sounded a little – peculiar." Her sole weakness is her penchant for things American. What rice to prepare for Spike's first dinner? "Uncle Ben's, of course, we got company!"

This avidity notwithstanding, the Puerto Rican society here seems possessed of a stronger character than the Italian, its more florid style perhaps an index of more foreign, that is, less corrupted, integrity. This, even though Spike, arriving at Red Hook, sees himself a missionary from "a more advanced civilization." He is, in a way, as he sets forth to clean up the neighborhood drug dealing with that icon of Americana, a baseball bat. But he represents a higher order only insofar as he himself accepts some outside authority over his own will. Otherwise the Hispanic characters seem stronger than the Italian because the latter are more Americanized (read: liberal, i.e., corrupt, bereft of moral fiber). Thus the contrasting "dives" in the first fights. Spike takes his loss in a "very smooth and professional" manner, as Cacetti compliments him. But when Spike wins a fix, the Puerto Rican Bandana transcends his loss by performing in an extravagant, baroque style, existentially asserting victory in the face of his dive. Sadly, Bandana disintegrates into drugs and fails to provide his sister with appropriate control. Yet both the Italian and Puerto Rican societies are distinguished from the white bread (or more appropriately, white-powder) Americana by having at least some inheritance of values and rule by custom.

The same contrast obtains between Spike's two women. The quiet, mysterious India asserts a weight that the airy Angel lacks. From Spike's perspective, his choice is between two exoticas. Angel represents his vertical class movement to a blonde class ideal, India a lateral movement to a more substantial worth. Beside India's integrity and care for Spike, Angel becomes a shallow aspiration. His marriage to India gives Spike fulfillment and maturity, in contrast to his comic heroism when he takes command in Red Hook. Banished from Bensonhurst, he seems enlarged by his crusading activities in Red Hook. But he is no more a savior than Angel is. In his police uniform at the end, Spike has grown into an emblem from a higher order.

Like *Mixed Blood,* this comic film explodes with a violent moment that is all the more shocking after the choreographed fights. Spike's hands are

Spike (Sasha Mitchell) of Bensonhurst tries to take his life into his own hands.

smashed in graphic close-up. This sudden physical punishment is necessary on two counts. Within the plot, it forever seals Spike's knowledge that his future is not in his own hands. He is a spike that others must hammer. In a wider sense, the scene reminds us that despite the film's comic tenor, its world is darkly shaded with pain, loss, and moral as well as social debts to be paid. The terrible lives of the drugged – graphically portrayed in both *Forty-Deuce* and *Mixed Blood* – shadow the sunnier lives of the Italian characters here. The comedy needs the jarring reality of that one torture scene.

The film subordinates the individual's interests to the collective good. This value transcends even traditional codes of honor. Nobody here questions the ethic of throwing a fight. On the contrary, the only issue is whether the thrower will receive his proper reward. When Spike abandons his career by refusing to take a dive, Morrissey exposes the individualist's delusion that there is integrity in independence.

The system's minor-key ruler, Cacetti, articulates the film's sharpest – and funniest – moral paradoxes. "You're an Italian," he advises Spike. "You gotta learn to go out into the world and make something of yourself." So he recommends Spike for a career in pirating porn videos, where the only moral imperative is not to confuse the kiddie and the hard-core labels.

Cacetti has gotten out of boxing because it has become "too lowlife, too –
ethnic." That is, it has become too black or Hispanic for the Americanized
Italian. Cacetti is flexible enough almost to accept the lesbianism of Spike's
mother: "At least she's not cheating on your father with another guy." He
accepts "all the women turning into dykes and tramps. But that's the way
it is in respectable society these days. And maybe we Italians have to accept
all that, but we don't have to like it." Now Cacetti is respectable himself:
"I even support the liberal politicians – all that garbage," he says, gesturing
at a wall photo of Mario Cuomo. One of these liberal politicians is a cartoon
Bella Abzug congresswoman (Sylvia Miles), whom we first meet collecting
money from Spike's numbers route. She uses a bar mitzvah platform to rail
against the violation of civil rights in the compulsory drug testing of teachers,
police officers, and fire fighters ("The first step towards a fascist takeover
of our democratic society"), then snorts coke in – where else? – a washroom,
indignant when her privacy is interrupted.

As does *Mixed Blood*, the film details an ethnic hierarchy. The Italian
subculture is more secure than the disintegrating Puerto Rican community,
which the Italian drug dealers exploit. India's mother believes that "if we
had the Mafia here instead of you useless police, we'd have plastic madonnas
in the yard instead of junkies." As in all Morrissey's films, true security,
freedom, and health derive from living within some laws.

Spike of Bensonhurst is a satire upon selfish appetites. The stolen food,
the drug dealing, the strategic sexuality, the political machinations in the
family/Family, all bespeak the characters' hunger for personal pleasure. As
Spike tells his mirror image, he has no interest in politics: "I'm just trying
to get a little piece of the pie." It is significant that Spike's craving for status
is expressed in terms of food. His large-scale ambition is imaged in his
continual grabbing of others' food: the accountant's pizza, the steak at
home, the steaks at the Cacettis'. Consequently, he is banished from the
two community banquets, the bar mitzvah, and Cacetti's dinner for Spike's
father. Though his first and friendliest scene with Cacetti ends with a home-
cooked meal, Spike's hands are mashed in the kitchen. Morrissey depicts
individualism and self-aggrandizement as petty appetites. Spike grows up
when he learns he can't nibble as he wants. He becomes most fully his own
man when he harnesses his hunger in the double uniform of the servant cop
and father. That lesson befalls everyone. When Borgnine's godfather figure
has his own strings pulled from higher up in the echelon, all illusions of
independence are dispelled.

This film may have the distinction of being America's first pro-Mafia film,
for it establishes the irregular forces of the criminal community as the

country's last bastion of moral values and social order. In effect, Morrissey whimsically elaborates on the matriarch's respect for the law and order of the Mafia. The police and politicians are characterized as helpless or corrupt. As Spike learns from his father, "What would happen in Bensonhurst if everybody ran around and did his own fuckin' thing? Ya wanna live in a toilet like Manhattan or the Bronx?" In this film a community manages to escape Morrissey's liberal toilet by accepting a social order and authority, albeit criminal, with a long tradition imported from Sicily. Morrissey got the idea for the film from reading of the popularity of John Gotti, an alleged racketeer, whose neighborhood threw a party for him when he was acquitted.

Morrissey considers *Spike* his "most political film of all with its blatant acknowledgement of the need for some kind of control, even gangster control, placed on life. Anything but the control – or lack of it – by the liberals. The stupidity of liberals leads to the lives in *Flesh* and *Trash* and *Heat*, the dead end of 'license.' " As Morrissey told Marcia Pally, "People who do whatever they want live in hell. This is the story of modern times."[10]

Though *Spike* is the lightest and most comical of Morrissey's three street films, the same themes emerge. The individual who strikes out for his own egotism has only a delusion of freedom. His liberty brings him destruction. "Real freedom requires controls and license outside controls is a kind of tyranny," says Morrissey. In all three films there is a tension between staying within one's geographical district and venturing beyond. As Crank was stymied by directions on how to get to Queens in *Forty-Deuce,* Thiago risks his life when he ventures beyond the Alphabet. Spike settles one gang fight over turf but establishes a new strength for himself when he is banished from Bensonhurst to Red Hook. His salvation, though, lies in his sanctioned return to his home territory. Not for Morrissey the romantic/liberal myth of the expansive quester. Rather, everyone is boxed in by cultural and geographic restrictions, or else destroys himself with delusions of authority.

The central male figures in the street films seem reversals of the Dallesandro figure in the *Flesh* trilogy. Instead of selling their sex, the later heroes try to exploit a system of more sophisticated corruption, the market of drugs and power. Yet they share the same bathetic flaw. All are hell-bent on feeding their easiest appetites.

Morrissey did not conceive of the three street films as a trilogy. "I never set out to make a series of films because it's a kind of miracle that I ever get one made. So I don't foresee follow-ups. But if I can do one more film and rework the material, then I do." The three street films began with place-name titles (*Mixed Blood* originally being *Alphabet City*) so their integrity and coherence should not surprise. In *Forty-Deuce* Morrissey establishes his subject, the vulnerable false family of the lost and the dissipated, a microcosmic view of the fine line that distinguishes the living from the dead in a world without moral bearings. In *Mixed Blood,* a larger budget and his own text examined the psychological losses of the obsolete family more closely and exposed the horror of the defiled vein and splattered street. In *Spike of Bensonhurst,* Morrissey drew back from the tragic to the comic vision. He allowed a character's redemption through submission to an albeit eccentric social order. Throughout the trilogy, Morrissey moves from hopeless alienation to a recovered community, from despair to hope, from bleak melodrama through tragedy to the sunnier heights of black comedy.

Two formal qualities lighten the films and suggest Morrissey's sympathy for even his most wrongheaded societies. One is his use of ethnic music. His choice has a moral base: "Rock and roll made drugs fashionable, and it is a twenty-four hour commercial for drug taking. Ethnic music, on the other hand, isn't negative or prodrug. It's life affirming, so I would rather use it in my films."[1] All three films have remarkable ethnic soundtracks. Morrissey's music – by Manu Dibango in *Forty-Deuce,* a variety of Puerto Rican songs with original additions by Andy Hernandez (of Kid Creole and the Coconuts) in *Mixed Blood,* and Italian and Spanish music by Coati Mundi in *Spike of Bensonhurst* – conveys the energy and character of cultural difference that the feature-film uses of jazz in Cassavetes's *Shadows* and Shirley Clarke's *The Cool World* did twenty years earlier. In *Mixed Blood,* if the predominant musical score represents Latino energy, it is framed by a plaintive ghetto theme that mourns the waste of life. In addition, however bleak or violent the plot events, or pathetic the characters, the music gives the films the upbeat tone of a comedy. Morrissey affirms the character of the subcultures even as he depicts their corruption by the American dream, by freedom. Morrissey finds more character in the ethnic bourgeoisie than in bohemian egotism.

The second formal quality that illuminates the street trilogy is the films' focus on spontaneous, sensitive, and often unpredictable performers. Morrissey hates

> acting-class acting, where you see all the effort behind the acting. Somehow it seems so appropriate an accompaniment to the phony liberal stories it usually presents. The phoniness of what passes for naturalistic acting nowadays is staggering. These affected "sincere"

efforts to be real, whether it's the stumbling Method or even Tom Cruise's gimmick of a "genuine" big smile on cue, seem to me bogus and artificial. I just stay away from most "serious" films now. But comedies in particular demand authenticity. Even to deal with contemporary life in a realistic way you need the artifice of comedy to succeed. I try to use spontaneous actors who never suggest to me that they are "acting," at least not in what passes for contemporary acting.

As he told Jay Scott, "I prefer 'people mannerisms' to 'actor mannerisms.' "[12] The street trilogy provides a textbook demonstration of Morrissey's dedication to an actor's cinema.

Mixed Blood is especially typical of Morrissey's success with a variety of untested performers. He spotted Rodney Harvey (José) in the street, a visitor from Philadelphia talking to a black kid. Two weeks before shooting began, Morrissey cast a Cuban delivery boy as Thiago when his original choice, a Brazilian acting student, dropped out to pursue his amateur soccer career in Japan. Richard Ulacia's speech is impeded by both his heavy Spanish accent and by his dyslexia, which causes syllabic displacements. So his Thiago became a more sympathetic and victimized character, a mix of strength and primitive vulnerability, yet with Cuban pride; the original Thiago fought his mother and (for example) ordered her to bring him the blonde Carol. These discoveries confirm Morrissey's "great confidence in my own intuition. I never tested anyone. I just know they can act." They blend in perfectly with experienced actors like Pedro Sanchez (Comanche) and Angel David (Juan the Bullet). Marilla Pera (Rita) came from a lengthy career of theater stardom, and from her international success as Sneli in Hector Babenco's *Pixote*. Though she could speak very little English at first, she appealed to Morrissey because she had made up her own dialogue in her earlier films.

Conclusion

Warhol's coterie considered Morrissey a sellout because he won the Factory its first (and only) large audience. But Morrissey's narrative orthodoxy did not make him a commercial director. On the contrary, his cinema rejects the commercial processes, both in its style and in its content.

The *Flesh* trilogy documents America's libertarianism with more realism and irony than even such respected commercial equivalents as *Midnight Cowboy* and *Easy Rider*. Morrissey denies the viewer any comfortable identification and any utopian possibility from the liberated libido. In his view, people who are freed from a social system are its most pathetic victims. For they become most easily commodified, turned into products for sale and trade. The sucking that the Dallesandro characters sell as sex becomes the sucking of the very lifeblood in the Dracula film. The sex bought and sold in the *Flesh* trilogy becomes the synthetic slaves in *Frankenstein*, then the synthetic "families," whether Menudo or Rita's, in *Mixed Blood*. Dracula's would-be brides are up-market versions of the street sex merchants, elevated in *L'Amour* but dropped in *Madame Wang's*, and more debased in *Forty-Deuce*. Sex and self seem opposed integrities in *Women in Revolt*, and indeed wherever sexuality defines the characters' relationships or their chosen form of freedom.

Morrissey deals with the commodity of cinema in the form of his films as well as in their content. Insofar as his films evoke a genre, they suggest that he might conform to some formal conventions. But his independence compels him to mischievously subvert his genre. Morrissey always affronts the commercial expectations of his form. So his (for the time) "hardcore" porn trilogy critiques the sexual liberty that it pretends to exercise/celebrate. His horror films assault the viewer with such graphic gore that the genre's coarseness becomes part of his subject. Morrissey denies us even the assurance of a genre's most ritual convention. In his "boxing" film the hero loses by winning. The street films have the language and music that would "sell" them to the very people who need – that is, need to be disturbed by – the films' lessons. If he uses a conventional form, it is to lure in the viewer for the subversive content. Morrissey's Beethoven, albeit historical, may well offend the lover of Beethoven's music. That is, Morrissey's most "arty" film attacks the conventional regard for the romantic artist. Instead of selling out, when Morrissey ventured into commercial cinema – whether popular horror, western, porn, fight flick, or art cinema – he challenged his audiences with wholly unsettling material. No Morrissey film would curry favor. The sudden shocks of violence in *Mixed Blood* and in *Spike* typify his calculated excess, as do his unfashionable moral and political conservatism.

Morrissey's works are so much of a piece that a consistent grid can be defined in the structure of all his personal films. In each we are led to identify with a central figure, usually a handsome young man. For five films he's the Dallesandro character; then he is Max, Lutz, Blow, Thiago, Karl, and finally Spike. These characters are always (in Rita's term) slow. Morrissey's antiromantic stance requires a "hero" who is neither quick of mind nor admirable of achievement, but a passive figure victimized by his own indulgence. In a world of demeaning values and debilitating liberty, he can aspire only to survive. Heroism is obsolete because aspiration and discipline are, as well.

This limited sensibility contrasts a more feminine figure possessed of greater self-knowledge, whose honesty wins our sympathy. This group includes Geri, Holly, Sally, Michael, the monkish Sasha, Esmerelda and her count, the maternal aspect of Rita, Karl's mother, and India. There is no such figure in the virtually all-male, hence despairing, *Forty-Deuce.* Morrissey's central dynamic contrasts a self-unaware male ego with a more sensible feminine counterpoise, whether a woman or a male of superior morality (such as Sasha or Dracula).

This tension is implicit even in the exceptions. In *Women in Revolt,* Morrissey focuses on the assertive sisterhood whose members (so to speak) regress into traditional (male-defined) roles. Here the women seek (but fail) to escape the male tyranny of Morrissey's "liberated" heroes. But as the rebel women are played by transvestites, the social tension has a psychological equivalent in which the male ego is superseded by the superior feminine. In *L'Amour* and *Madame Wang's,* as they are cross-cultural satires, the sensitivity is not in the women but in the central men. Michael must develop his; the East German has been trained to resist modern American values.

In each film the hero encounters either helpful or obstructive figures of power. In the *Flesh* trilogy, Joe is commodified by his customers' power as he wastes his preferable relationships with Geri, Holly, and Sally. In the horror comedies, the servant Joe is Everyman, asserting a respectable personal code against a supernatural evil. In contrast, Otto and Anton serve self-aggrandizing, nightmarish masters. Karl van Beethoven has two benign facilitators, the actress and his mother, but his lover surrenders him and he fails in a crucial moment to support his mother. Failing to mature, he loses both women. Though remaining in his uncle's thrall, he fails to accept its positive aspect. Ludwig van Beethoven is closer to the horror monsters than to the handsome young hero.

There are telling variations on this motif in the street films. In all three there are powers behind the powers, often invisible manipulators of the visible authorities. In *Forty-Deuce*, Mr. Roper is assumed to be the facilitator but proves impotent, a token of the socioeconomic system rather than an active will. Augie, the oppressor, stands in for the more formidable Mike. All three are negative alternatives to any sustaining feminine. In *Mixed Blood*, Rita is both Thiago's facilitator, as she guides his life and fortunes, and his oppressor, as she delimits his maturation. Spike's facilitator, Cacetti, represents the need and reward for social submission. Spike is prevented by his own headstrong ego, which we see him forced to overcome. His proper rebellion (like Karl's, Blow's, and that of the women in revolt) is not against the authority figure (here Cacetti and *his* superior) but against his own will.

Each hero is defined by the values of his quest. In Morrissey's view of our world, however, few quests have a noble objective. *Flesh* – as we learn from Joe's customers as much as from his scene with his baby – is about the need for a relationship that would transcend the physical. But (as in *Forty-Deuce*, *Women in Revolt*, *L'Amour* and *Madame Wang's*) the only relationship the characters know is sex – the tie that commodifies. In *Trash*, the objective is self-respect (Holly the prime definer), with welfare support the means; Joe's deadening by drugs is the negative parody. In *Heat*, the characters use the hope of a career – whether in show business, motel management or living off of a walking checkbook – as the means to that Hollywood speciality, romance. In *Forty-Deuce* and *Mixed Blood*, sex and drugs are the means to money and survival. Beethoven's nephew seeks independence, but mainly through (and for) sex.

The monsters, especially Frankenstein and Dracula, seek dominance over others to avert mortality. The former's quest is undermined by the sexual license of his kindred wife. The latter parallels the Di Fioris' need for a marriage to renew themselves, but only in nonmoral terms. Like Michael, the minor-key composer in *L'Amour,* the mad Beethoven needs supportive affection as he ages. But the celebrity's power turns him into a self-destructive tyrant, a fate from which the quite incompetent Michael is saved.

Rather than heroic quests, Morrissey's characters are propelled by their mundane appetites. From Joe's cupcake, the hungers "grow" to include unnatural sex, the deadening anodyne of drugs, indiscriminate hungers (Jessie's "you name it, I'll eat it"), Frankenstein's and Dracula's lust for power over sex and death, and overall, from all of these male hustlers, from Joe through Spike, dominance over others. Spike's feral nature seems best expressed in his theft of both food and women. Outside of this film, Morrissey shows relatively few eating scenes; his characters know so little community that sex and drugs have become their consuming hungers. Perhaps we see Spike eat so often because he is Morrissey's only hero who achieves (albeit secular) salvation.

Related to the value of this sanctioned appetite, the most striking consistency in Morrissey's work is the range of family represented. There are often real family relationships, but even more false-family figures, such as the pseudomaternal Lydia in *Heat* or the false parent Roper in *Forty-Deuce.* The false families represent delusions of security and value. Even the real family figure may be a figure of betrayal, for example, Jessie, Holly's sister, Joe's wife, the marquise, Uncle Ludwig, and/or Karl. Stingray's absent family in *Mixed Blood* exerts a positive influence that Mitchell's absent father in *Forty-Deuce* fails to provide. Rita La Punta may seem a supportive mother figure to her boys, but she is false to her real son by misdirecting his life. Spike learns to be content with the family that accepts him and stops trying to crash the Cacettis.

In fact, the family is Morrissey's central metaphor. It ideally represents a base of emotional support, understanding, and moral guidance. The teen-gang false families may provide forms of the first two criteria but fail in the third. The family also represents the larger social unit insofar as it requires submission and should provide discipline and moral exemplars. A Morrissey character's true strength is defined by his or her ability to sustain a proper familial relationship. This makes Max and Michael's desire to become a family in *L'Amour* a key to the canon – especially given their horrid antagonisms. Alternatively, the dread self-indulgents seek independence from commitments and control, disregarding their obligations to others, whether the family or society. This distinguishes the trashed Joe from his committed Holly, as it did earlier the obliging Joe from his exploiting wife.

Despite the consistency of his moral vision, in the auteurist age Morrissey was a director who did not appear to direct. Instead, he entrusted his performers with developing their own characters. In this sense, from the outset he denied the vanity of the romantic artist. One advantage of Morrissey's respect for his performers is that his films transcend his politics. Their emotional and visceral impact surpasses their "moral." So despite Morrissey's dogmatic conservatism, he has produced, in John Russell Taylor's words, "a cinema of complete human acceptance: however odd the characters are, they are never patronized, never made fun of, never presented as material for a quick camp giggle.... Morrissey belongs to that select band who make films in such a way that the film becomes a transparent envelope, through which we can enter, telepathically, their minds."[1] This makes Morrissey's bleak satires radically humanist. Morrissey shared Jean Renoir's trust in the improvisational grace of his (quite different) actors. But he also shared the moral embrace that Renoir articulated as Octave in *The Rules of the Game* (1939): "You see, on this earth, there is one thing which is terrible, and that is that everyone has their own good reasons."[2]

Whatever his sources, Morrissey has exerted a remarkable influence. On the one hand, his aesthetic of improvisational discovery nourished the rich vein of film docudrama that includes Alan King, Jim McBride, Dennis Hopper, Norman Mailer, Shirley Clarke, and Robert Kramer. On the other hand, his cinema of humanist eccentricity can be traced on into the work of Robert Frank and the films of Jonas and Adolfos Mekas, Albert Brooks, Jim Jarmusch, Henry Jaglom, Jonathan Demme, and the Coens, all of which together form arguably the liveliest tributary in contemporary American film.

Be that as it may, Paul Morrissey stands alone in American cinema as the independent's independent. In the language of his favorite director, Carol Reed, Morrissey is an outcast from all the islands, from the independent to the commercial, a man between, an odd man out, with no camp (in either sense) safe from his subversion. Yet so bracing and compassionate are the epiphanies of this reactionary conservative's films, that they can speak to and for even a dread liberal (such as the author).

Notes

Introduction

1. John Russell Taylor, *Directors & Directions: Cinema for the Seventies* (London: Eyre Methuen, 1975), p. 165.

2. On the movement see Blaine Allan, "The Beat, The Hip, and The Square," in *Film Reader 5* (Evanston, Ill.: Northwestern University Press, 1982), pp. 257–68; and David E. James, *Allegories of Cinema: American Film in the Sixties* (Princeton, N.J.: Princeton University Press, 1989), pp. 86–100.

3. Unless otherwise attributed, all Morrissey quotations are from interviews with the author.

4. For example, ex-superstar Ondine says, "The people that offended me at the Factory were not the Andy. It was Morrissey that was offensive. . . . He was so, you know . . . he was just coming from a different. . . . The thing that shocked me the most was when [Warhol] started to leave off being his own personal representative and allowed people like Morrissey . . . to take over the control." From Patrick S. Smith, *Warhol: Conversations about the Artist* (Ann Arbor: UMI Research Press, 1988), pp. 278–9. Stephen Koch quotes a more coherent Ondine: "Paul is a garbage collector. . . . He's taken the art out of Warhol, which is something you can't do" (*Stargazer: Andy Warhol's World and His Films* [New York: Praeger, 1973], p. 102). On "Morrissey the wicked stepmother" see David Bourdon, *Warhol* (New York: Abrams, 1989), p. 300.

5. Quoted in Jean Stein, *Edie: An American Biography* (New York: Dell, 1982), p. 167. In Viva's transparent "novel," *Superstar* (New York: Putnam, 1970), Morrissey is presented as "Fred Morris, A's right-hand man" (p. 98) and characterized by his antagonism to drug use (p. 253).

6. Koch, *Stargazer*, p. 80.

7. P. Adams Sitney, *Visionary Film: The American Avant-Garde* (New York: New York University Press, 1978), p. 371.

8. Koch, *Stargazer*, p. 100.

9. Though the sale grossed an astonishing $25,333,368, the materials ranged crazily in quality and worth. For example, Warhol's large collection of cookie tins and other varieties of kitsch obviously sold high for their celebrity association.

10. Tony Rayns, "Death at Work: Evolution and Entropy in Factory Films," in

Michael O'Pray, ed., *Andy Warhol Film Factory* (London: British Film Institute, 1989) p. 169.

11. Taylor, *Directors and Directions*, pp. 137–8, 154.

12. Madeleine Harmsworth, review, *Sunday Mirror*, April 4, 1971.

13. For example, see Albie Thoms, *Polemics for a New Cinema* (Sydney: Wild & Woolley, 1978), p. 29.

14. David James, "The Producer as Author," in O'Pray, *Andy Warhol*, p. 141. The paper is reprinted in James, *Allegories of Cinema*. See also Parker Tyler, *The Shadow of an Airplane Climbs the Empire State Building: A World Theory of Film* (New York: Anchor, 1972), pp. 236–44.

15. Peter Wollen, "Raiding the Icebox," in O'Pray, *Andy Warhol*, pp. 19, 21.

16. Koch, *Stargazer*, p. 33.

17. Ibid., pp. 49–50. Cf. Viva, "Viva and God," Voice Art Supplement, *Village Voice*, May 5, 1987, p. 9: "*Blue Movie*, entirely my idea, and enthusiastically seconded by Andy, was the occasion of so much embarrassment to Paul Morrissey that he could not stay on the set and watch the filming.... it was the only film made solely by Andy and the actors (Louie Waldon and I), and no one else had a single thing to say or made a single move in its direction." The screenplay has been published as Andy Warhol, *Blue Movie* (New York: Grove, 1970).

18. Parker Tyler, *Underground Film: A Critical History* (London: Penguin, 1971), pp. 41–2, 90–1. On Morrissey's advances see pp. 178–9.

19. Ibid., pp. 144, 173–4.

20. In Charles Thomas Samuels, *Encountering Directors* (New York: Putnam, 1972), p. 32.

21. David Ehrenstein, "The Filmmaker as Homosexual Hipster: Andy Warhol Contextualized," *Arts Magazine* (Summer 1989), 64.

22. Koch, *Stargazer*, p. 105.

23. Joseph Gelmis, *The Film Director as Superstar* (New York: Doubleday, 1970), pp. 66–7.

24. Bourdon, *Warhol*, p. 414.

25. Paul Gardner, "Morrissey Gives the Director's View," *New York Times* (November 14, 1972).

26. F. William Howton, "Filming Andy Warhol's *Trash*," *Filmmakers Newsletter*, 5, no. 8 (June 1972), 24.

27. Taylor, *Directors and Directions*, p. 137.

28. Howton, "Filming *Trash*," p. 24.

29. Gardner, "Morrissey."

30. Taylor, *Directors and Directions*, p. 138.

31. Kathy Acker, "Blue Valentine," in O'Pray, *Andy Warhol*, p. 65.

32. Quoted in Patrick S. Smith, *Andy Warhol's Art and Films* (Ann Arbor, Mich.: UMI Research Press, 1986), p. 193.

33. Quoted by Jonas Mekas, "Notes After Reseeing the Movies of Andy Warhol," in O'Pray, *Andy Warhol*, p. 33.

34. Bourdon, *Warhol*, p. 294. See also Tyler, *Underground Film*, pp. 29–30. Later Warhol hired Dallesandro's brother as his driver.

35. Gavin Lambert, *On Cukor* (New York: Capricorn, 1973), p. 154.

36. Andy Warhol and Pat Hackett, *Popism: The Warhol '60s* (New York: Harper and Row, 1980), p. 239.

37. Paul Morrissey, *Dialogue on Film*, American Film Institute, 4, no. 2 (November 1974), p. 23.

38. Howton, "Filming *Trash*," p. 24.

39. Quoted in Marcia Pally, "The New York Newsday Interview with Paul Morrissey," *Newsday* (February 2, 1989).

40. Helen Knode, "That 'L' Word," *L.A. Weekly* (November 18–24, 1988), 45.

41. James, *Allegories of Cinema*, p. 90.

42. Gregory Battcock, "Four Films by Andy Warhol," in O'Pray, *Andy Warhol*, p. 46.

43. Koch, *Stargazer*, p. 122.

44. James, *Allegories of Cinema*, p. 79.

45. Viva, "Viva and God," 9.

46. Louis Marcorelles, *Living Cinema: New Directions in Contemporary Film-Making* (London: George Allen and Unwin, 1973), p. 83.

47. Morrissey, *Dialogue on Film*, p. 20.

48. James, *Allegories of Cinema*, p. 71.

49. Ibid., p. 91.

50. Charles Michener, "Put-on Artist," *Newsweek* (September 23, 1974), 90.

51. Tony Rayns, "Andy Warhol Films Inc: Communication in Action," *Cinema* (U.K.), 6–7 (August 1970), 45.

52. Quoted in Koch, *Stargazer*, p. 80.

53. On Stan Brakhage's shorter rebellion against the film–drug connection see Tyler, *Underground Film*, p. 32.

54. Gardner, "Morrissey."

55. The book collection attracted Judith Thurman's report, "Paul Morrissey: A World of Images," in *Architectural Digest* (May 1990), 72–8.

1. The Life and Work

1. Koch lists some of the surprisingly many Factory denizens who were refugees from Catholicism (*Stargazer*, p. 11). Viva remembers Warhol as not so much a father confessor as a father-surrogate "attention-giver" who encouraged his entourage to perform: "The Factory was a way for a group of Catholics to purge themselves of Catholic repression ... and Catholic repression in the fifties was so extreme that the only way to liberate oneself from it was to react in the completely opposite direction, and then hopefully to level off after that" (in Jean Stein, *Edie*, p. 176). Rayns raises their common Catholicism and "a detached fascination with the blatantly immoral behaviour of the Factory crowd" as possible reasons why Warhol "surrendered" to Morrissey (O'Pray, *Andy Warhol*, p. 167).

2. *Film Culture*, no. 37 (Summer 1965), insert, 49.

3. Donald Lyons, "One-Way Ticket to Morrisseyville," *Details* (November 1988), 173.

4. O'Pray, *Andy Warhol*, p. 167. Warhol recounts his early experiences with Morrissey in Warhol and Hackett, *Popism*, pp. 117–19, 262–5.

5. Victor Bockris and Gerard Malanga, *Up-tight: The Velvet Underground Story* (London: Omnibus, 1983), p. 11. David Bourdon presents Warhol as more responsible for conceiving and completing the idea than was Morrissey (Bourdon, *Warhol*, pp. 218–22). See also Warhol and Hackett, *Popism*, pp. 143–6. In 1990, Velvet veterans John Cale and Lou Reed elegized Warhol in a fifteen-song cycle, *Songs for Drella*. On the aesthetic revolution in such countercultural festivals and their relation to underground film see James, *Allegories of Cinema*, pp. 133–7.

6. Bockris and Malanga, *Up-tight*, p. 31.

7. Marshall McLuhan and Quentin Fiore, *The Medium is the Massage: An Inventory of Effects* (New York: Bantam, 1967), unpaginated.

8. Jonas Mekas, "Movie Journal," *Village Voice* (September 29, 1966), 27.

9. Andrew Sarris, "Films: *The Chelsea Girls*," *Village Voice* (December 15, 1966), 33.

10. On the various receptions of *The Chelsea Girls* see Bourdon, *Warhol*, pp. 248–9, 254.

11. Ibid., p. 247.

12. Parker Tyler, *Screening the Sexes: Homosexuality in the Movies* (New York: Holt, Rinehart and Winston, 1973), pp. 188–9. Cf. Tyler, *Underground Film*, pp. 212–16.

13. Lambert, *On Cukor*, p. 154.

14. Quoted in *Variety* (August 13, 1969).

15. Margia Kramer, *Andy Warhol et al.: The FBI File on Andy Warhol* (New York: UnSub Press, 1988), pp. 35–7. For Warhol's recollections of the film see Warhol and Hackett, *Popism*, pp. 259–62.

16. John Simon, *Reverse Angle: A Decade of American Films* (New York: Potter, 1982), p. 316. Sarris, "Films," leveled the same charge against *Lonesome Cowboys*.

17. Morrissey can be seen briefly in the background of the party scene, but the only entourage member featured in the scene is Viva as the underground filmmaker-hostess. Morrissey also appears in the Malibu party scene in George Cukor's *Rich and Famous*, along with Christopher Isherwood and Roger Vadim.

18. For a significant contemporary appreciation of *Flesh* see John Weightman, "Flesh in the Afternoon," *Encounter* (June 1970), 30–2.

19. David Robinson, "When is a Dirty Film . . . ?" *Sight and Sound* (Winter 1971–2), 30.

20. Morrissey, *Dialogue on Film*, p. 22.

21. David Curtis, *Experimental Cinema* (New York: Dell, 1971), p. 180.

22. James, *Allegories of Cinema*, p. 77.

23. Morrissey, *Dialogue on Film*, p. 21.

24. Lambert, *On Cukor*, pp. 153–4.

25. Koch, *Stargazer*, pp. 61, 77.

26. Tyler, *Shadow*, pp. 239, 243.

27. Helen Knode, "That 'L' Word," p. 45.

2. The Flesh Trilogy

1. On Morrissey's treatment of the figure see Tyler, *Screening the Sexes*, pp. 54–8.

2. Morrissey, *Dialogue on Film*, pp. 24–5.

3. James, *Allegories of Cinema*, p. 68.

4. Andy Warhol, *The Andy Warhol Diaries*, ed. Pat Hackett (New York: Warner, 1989), p. 439.

5. Bourdon, *Warhol*, p. 296.

6. On Dallesandro's passivity see James, *Allegories of Cinema*, pp. 78–9.

7. Margaret Tarratt, "Flesh," *Films and Filming* (April 1970), 43.

8. James, *Allegories of Cinema*, p. 79.

9. Gene Youngblood, *Expanded Cinema* (New York: Dutton, 1970), p. 117.

10. Paul Arthur, "Flesh of Absence," in O'Pray, p. 150.

11. Bourdon, *Warhol*, p. 296.

12. James, "The Producer as Author," in O'Pray, *Andy Warhol*, pp. 142–3.

13. Greg Ford, " 'You name it, I'll eat it,' " *Cinema* (L.A.), no. 33 (Spring 1973), 32.

14. Jonas Mekas, *Movie Journal: The Rise of the New American Cinema, 1959–1971* (New York: Collier, 1972), p. 332.

15. Weightman, "Flesh," 32.

16. Of course, Morrissey's reference is to the Fillmore Auditorium, a huge old theater on Second Avenue and Sixth Street, a popular venue for rock shows and therefore for drug dealing.

17. Quoted in Scott Winokur, "*Fusion* Interview: Paul Morrissey," *Fusion*, no. 50 (February 19, 1971), 13.

18. Quoted in Howton, "Filming *Trash*," 25.

19. Marsha Kinder and Beverle Houston, *Close-Up: A Critical Perspective on Film* (New York: Harcourt Brace Jovanovich, 1972), pp. 241–2.

20. Ibid., p. 237.

21. Melton S. Dawes, "Morrissey – From *Flesh* and *Trash* to *Blood for Dracula*," *New York Times* (July 15, 1973).

22. John Weightman, "All Flesh is Trash," *Encounter* (June 1971), 45–6.

23. Kinder and Houston, *Close-Up*, p. 242.

24. Warhol told Ralph Pomeroy (in "An Interview with Andy Warhol," *Afterimage*, no. 2 [Autumn 1970], 38) that Sklar was just brought in off the street for this debut. But Morrissey recalls that Sklar was an aspiring actor who was introduced by Andy's oldest friend, Suzy Frankfort, Sklar's cousin. He did so well that he was featured in *L'Amour*, by which time he also had a successful jewelry business. "Andy could never remember anything correctly," Morrissey explains. "He was always getting things mixed up. In interviews he'd usually agree with whatever anyone, especially the journalists, said, or what he guessed they wanted him to say."

25. Guy Flatley, "He Enjoys Being a Girl," *New York Times* (November 15, 1970).

26. John Russell Taylor, "Paul Morrissey/*Trash*," *Sight and Sound* (Winter 1971–2), 32. For a less sympathetic review see Pauline Kael, *Deeper Into Movies* (New York: Little Brown, 1973), pp. 153–7.

27. See Annette Kuhn, "Sexual Disguise and the Cinema," in *The Power of the Image: Essays on Representation and Sexuality* (London: Routledge & Kegan Paul, 1985), pp. 48–73.

28. Taylor, "Paul Morrissey/*Trash*," 31.

29. Tarratt, "Flesh," p. 43.

30. Quoted by Winokur, "*Fusion* Interview," 13.

31. Kinder and Houston, *Close-Up*, p. 242.

32. Greg Ford, "*Trash*," in *Cinema* (L.A.), 7, no. 2 (Spring 1972), 55.

33. Contrary to David James, "The Producer as Author," in O'Pray, *Andy Warhol*, pp. 141–2.

34. Morrissey, *Dialogue on Film*, p. 29.

35. John Weightman, "Minimal Relationships," *Encounter* (June 1973), 37–9.

36. Marsha Kinder and Beverle Houston, "Woman and Manchild in the Land of Broken Promise: Ken Russell's *Savage Messiah* and Paul Morrissey's *Heat*," in *Women and Film*, 1, nos. 3–4 (1973), 36–7.

37. Ford, "You Name It," 35.

38. Yvette Biro, *Profane Mythology: The Savage Mind of the Cinema*, trans. Imre Goldstein (Bloomington: Indiana University Press, 1982), p. 98.

39. Pauline Kael, *5001 Nights at the Movies* (New York: Holt, Rinehart and Winston, 1982), p. 246.

40. Joan Mellen, *Women and their Sexuality in the New Film* (New York: Horizon, 1973), p. 100.

41. Paul Gardner, "Morrissey Gives the Director's View," *New York Times* (November 14, 1972).

42. For a contrary reading of increasing misogyny across the trilogy, see Kinder and Houston, "Woman and Manchild," pp. 31–7.

43. Morrissey, *Dialogue on Film*, pp. 30–1.

3. Approaching Politics

1. Harris Dienstfrey, "The New American Cinema," *Commentary*, 6, no. 33 (June 1962), 499. See also David James, *Allegories of Cinema*, pp. 96–7.

2. Ken Kelman, "Anticipations of the Light," *The Nation* (May 11, 1964), 412–13. Kelman's other two main categories in this "spiritual medium" he describes as "films of liberation, films which suggest, mainly through anarchic fantasy, the possibilities of the human spirit in its socially uncorrupted state," and "mythically oriented" cinema that addresses our "need to fill our rationalistic void."

3. In prerelease reports, *Women in Revolt* was referred to under various other titles, such as *Sex, Andy Warhol's PIGS*, and *Andy Warhol's Women*. Jackie Curtis attests to Morrissey's control of the film ("It would have been better if Paul Morrissey left his two fucking cents out.") in Patrick S. Smith, *Andy Warhol's Art and Films* (Ann Arbor, Mich.: UMI Research Press, 1986), p. 272. Ed McCormack describes Morrissey's direction in "Only PIGS Could Follow Trash," *Inter/VIEW*, 2, no. 2 (1972), 23–5.

4. Stein, *Edie*, p. 226.

5. On the relation of feminism to the American underground cinema, see James, *Allegories of Cinema*, pp. 304–45.

6. The film was originally intended as a vehicle for Holly Woodlawn, to reward her for her triumph in *Trash*. But with Holly impeded by alcoholism at the time, the film was hijacked by the scene-chewing performances of Candy Darling and Jackie Curtis. This backstage gossip only confirms a point: Morrissey invests his films in his performers.

7. Ford, " 'You name it,' " 31. Cf. Stuart Byron, "Reactionaries in Radical Drag," *Village Voice* (March 16, 1972), 69.

8. Tyler, *Screening the Sexes,* pp. 230–1.

9. James, *Allegories of Cinema,* p. 79.

10. Tyler, *Screening the Sexes,* p. 231.

11. On the very personal element in Candy's impersonations, see Bourdon, *Warhol,* p. 296.

12. Byron, "Reactionaries," 69.

13. Bourdon, *Warhol,* p. 316.

14. Kael, *5001 Nights,* p. 660.

15. *The Time Out Film Guide,* ed. Tom Milne (London: Penguin, 1989), p. 664.

16. William Wolf, "From *Trash* to Riches," *Cue* (November 14, 1970), 13.

17. Ford, p. 31.

18. J. Mekas, "Notes," 14.

19. Jean-Luc Godard, *Weekend/Wind From the East* (New York: Simon and Schuster, 1972), p. 164.

4.   *The Costume Films*

1. Dawes, "Morrissey."

2. Morrissey, *Dialogue on Film,* p. 21.

3. Michener, "Put-on Artist," 90.

4. Carter Ratcliff, *Andy Warhol* (New York: Abbeville Modern Masters, 1983), p. 104. Nevertheless, Ratcliff does call Morrissey Warhol's alter-ego in his filmmaking activities, and states that Morrissey "directed" all Warhol films after 1968. That includes *Blue Movie* (p. 126), which he didn't. Furthermore, Morrissey's two horror films did extremely, not "moderately," well.

5. Paul Zimmerman, "*Andy Warhol's Frankenstein,*" *Newsweek* (May 20, 1974), 105.

6. Tyler, *Underground Film,* p. 67.

7. Dawes, "Morrissey."

8. Ibid.

9. Walter Evans, "Monster Movies: A Sexual Theory," in *Movies as Artifacts: Cultural Criticism of Popular Film,* ed. Michael T. Marsden, John G. Nachbar, and Sam L. Grogg, Jr. (Chicago: Nelson-Hall, 1982), pp. 129–36.

10. Ibid., p. 134.

11. Bernardo Bertolucci, *Last Tango in Paris* (New York: Dell Publishing, 1973), p. 160.

12. Morrissey, *Dialogue on Film,* p. 23.

13. This emphasis recalls Hitchcock's unconventional use of depth in *Dial M for Murder* (1954), where the technique was not used for projectiles out of the screen so much as to suggest vulnerable balances within the frame.

14. Morrissey, *Dialogue on Film,* p. 28.

15. Ibid., pp. 26–7.

16. Morrissey to F. William Howton, quoted in "Filming Andy Warhol's *Trash,*" *Filmmaker's Newsletter,* 5, no. 8 (June 1972), 25.

17. There seems to be a playful joke at Andy *Warhola's* expense when the marquis

assures his family of the historical safeness of anyone whose surname ends in *ula*. This of the enigmatic white-haired spirit we watched paintbrush his hair black in the credit sequence. Warhol is called Drella, a combination of Cinderella and Dracula, in his tape-transcript novel, *a* (New York: Grove Press, 1968). Similarly, in *Flesh for Frankenstein*, a busty madam is called Viva. Morrissey denies being aware of either joke.

18. The other players at the tavern table are writer-actor Gerard Brasch and Andrew Braunberg, who produced Polanski's *Macbeth* and *What?* The latter was originally planned for shooting in 3-D but at the last minute Polanski rejected the idea as inappropriate. Polanski proposed Morrissey and *Frankenstein* to the producers.

19. Morrissey, *Dialogue on Film*, p. 25.

20. Ibid., p. 27.

21. The film's American release was delayed for two years. Morrissey battled the producers in the French courts over the ownership of the work print. Ultimately the final editing was settled by an arbitrator. The first reel suffered the most from the producers' interference, but Morrissey was able to restore the first and last twenty minutes before the American release.

22. The Brakhage-Warhol antithesis has often been enunciated. See Tyler, *Underground Film*, pp. 32–4, 207–8, for an early treatment. For the fullest recent one, see James, *Allegories of Cinema*, chapters 2–3.

23. Morrissey to Matthew Flamm, "*Trash*-ing Beethoven," *New York Post* (June 9, 1988), 35.

24. Ibid.

25. Helen Knode, "Sweet Bird of Youth," *L.A. Weekly* (July 17, 1988), p. 45.

5. The Street Life

1. Kevin Bacon was fresh from his success in *Friday the 13th* but *Diner* was not yet released. He won an Obie for his stage performance as Ricky.

2. The play had enjoyed a production a year earlier, then had a three-week run off-Broadway.

3. Morrissey did not notice the Fierstein poster and does not recall the Marlboro one. Still, the effects register.

4. See Tyler, *Underground Film*, pp. 188–9.

5. Jonathan Rosenbaum, *Film: The Front Line* (Denver: Arden, 1983), p. 215.

6. From an interview by Gary Indiana, in "Aces the Deuce: An Interview with Paul Morrissey," *East Village Eye* (March 1983), 8.

7. Arthur, "Flesh of Absence," in O'Pray, *Andy Warhol*, p. 149.

8. This recalls the use of the playground for the gang rumble in Shirley Clarke's *The Cool World* (1963).

9. John Kobal, "Paul Morrissey: Life After Warhol," *Films and Filming* (June 1986), 17.

10. Pally, "Newsday Interview."

11. Interview of Morrissey by William Gibbons, "Conscience of a Post-Warhol Conservative," *Movieline* (November 4, 1988), 37.

12. Jay Scott, "The wacky, irreverent orbit of Paul Morrissey," (Toronto) *Globe and Mail* (November 11, 1988).

Conclusion

1. Taylor, *Directors and Directions*, p. 32.
2. Jean Renoir, *The Rules of the Game* (London: Lorrimer, 1970), p. 53.

Filmography

Unless otherwise noted, all films are American releases.

Films by Paul Morrissey

1961
Ancient History, 5 minutes.

Dream and Day Dream, 6 minutes.

1962
Mary Martin Does It, 16 minutes.
Cast: Robin Brooks, Ellie Harvey.

Civilization and Its Discontents, 45 minutes.
Cast: Marco St. John, Robin Brooks, Jared Martin, Pierre Blanchard, Virginia Bell.

1963
Taylor Mead Dances, 14 minutes.
Cast: Taylor Mead, Katherine Roberts, Roberts Blossom.

1964
Peaches and Cream, 5.5 minutes.
Assistant: Charles Levine.
Music: Louis Masagni.
Paintings: Stanley Fisher.

Like Sleep, 14 minutes.

Sleep Walk, 70 minutes.
Cast: Pierre Blanchard, Jennifer Salt, Maurice Braddell.

Merely Children, 10 minutes. Silent.
Cast: Gina Fisher, Nicholas Gilman, Marla Fisher.

About Face, 9 minutes. Silent.
Cast: Karen Holzer.

The Origin of Captain America, 10 minutes. Silent.
Cast: Joseph Diaz.

1965
All Aboard the Dreamland Choo-Choo
Cast: Richard Toelk.

My Hustler, 70 minutes. Sound.
Producer, camera operator: Andy Warhol.
Production assistant: Morrissey.
Cast: Paul America (young hustler), Ed Hood (the john), Joseph Campbell (Sugar Plum Fairy), John MacDermott (houseboy), Genevieve Charbon (neighbor), Dorothy Dean (oriental woman).

1966 ··
The Chelsea Girls, 3 hrs. 15 minutes, two screens.
Director: Morrissey.
Producer, camera operator: Andy Warhol.
Music: The Velvet Underground.
Cast: *"The Gerard Malanga Story": Marie Mencken, Mary Woronov, Gerard Malanga.
  "Hanoi Hanna (queen of China)": Mary Woronov, International Velvet, Ingrid Superstar, Angelina "Pepper" Davis.
  "The Pope Ondine Story": Bob "Ondine" Olivio, Angelina Davis, Ingrid Superstar, Albert Rene Ricard, Mary Woronov, International Velvet, Ronna.
  "The John": Ed Hood, Patrick Flemming, Mario Montez, Angelina Davis, International Velvet, Mary Woronov, Gerard Malanga, Rene Ricard, Ingrid Superstar.
  "Their Town": Eric Emerson.
Episode order at Cinémathèque premiere, Sept. 15, 1966: The Pope Ondine Story. The Gerard Malanga Story. George's Room. Hanoi Hanna. Afternoon. The John. The Trip. The Closet.

1967
**** (Four Stars),** 25 hours.
Segments: **International Velvet** (30 min., with Alan Midgette, Dickins Ackerman); **Alan and Dickins** (2 hours, with Midgette, Ackerman); **Imitation of Christ** (8 hours, with Patrick Tilden, Nico, Ondine, Tom Baker, Taylor Mead, Bridgid Polk); **Courtroom** (30 min., with Ondine, Ivy, Ultra Violet, Rene Ricard); **Gerard Has His Hair Removed with Nair** (30 min., with Gerard Malanga, four girls); **Katrina Dead** (30 min., with Rene Ricard, Ondine); **Sausalito** (30 min., with Nico); **Alan and Apple**

---

*As in the other Warhol/Morrissey "experiments," these names were can labels to identify the footage, not titles.

(with Alan Midgette); *Group One* (30 min.); *Sunset Beach on Long Island* (30 min.); *Haight-Ashbury* (30 min., with Ultra Violet, Ondine, Nico); *Tiger Morse* (20 min.); nineteen other 30-minute reels.

The Loves of Ondine, 86 minutes. Sound.
Cast: Ondine, Viva, Joe Dallesandro, Angelina Davis, Ivy Nicholson, Bridgid Polk. (Scenes from **** shown as a separate feature.)

I, a Man, 100 minutes. Sound.
Cast: Tom Baker, Ivy Nicholson, Ingrid Superstar, Valerie Solanis, Cynthia May, Betina Coffin, Ultra Violet, Nico.

Bike Boy, 96 minutes. Color. Sound.
Cast: Joe Spencer (the bike boy), Viva (girl on couch), Ed Hood (florist), Bridget Polk (girl with husband), Ingrid Superstar (girl in kitchen), George Ann, Bruce Ann (sales assistants), Clay Bird, Bettina Coffin, Valerie Solanis.

Lonesome Cowboys, 110 minutes.
Director: Morrissey.
Producer, camera operator: Andy Warhol.
Cast: Taylor Mead (nurse), Viva (Ramona D'Alvarez), Louis Waldon (Mickey), Eric Emerson (Eric), Joe Dallesandro (Little Joe), Julian Burroughs (Brother), Alan Midgette (Alan), Tom Hompertz (Julian), Frances Francine (sheriff).

1968
Flesh, 105 minutes.
Director, story, screenplay, photography, camera operator, editor: Morrissey.
Producer: Andy Warhol.
Cast: Joe Dallesandro (Joe), Geraldine Smith (Joe's wife), Maurice Braddell (artist), Louis Waldon (gymnast), Geri Miller (Geri), Candy Darling and Jackie Curtis (friends), Patti d'Arbanville (wife's girlfriend), Barry Brown (boy on street), John Christian (young patron).

1970
Trash, 103 minutes.
Director, story, screenplay, photography, camera operator: Morrissey.
Producer: Andy Warhol.
Editor: Jed Johnson, Morrissey.
Song: "Mama Look at Me Now" by Joe Saggarino, sung by Geri Miller.
Sound: Jed Johnson.
Cast: Joe Dallesandro (Joe), Holly Woodlawn (Holly), Jane Forth (Jane), Michael Sklar (welfare investigator), Geri Miller (go-go dancer), Andrea Feldman (rich girl), Johnny Putnam (boy from Yonkers), Bruce Pecheur (Jane's husband), Diane Podlewski (Holly's sister), Bob Dallesandro (boy on street).

1971
Women in Revolt, 97 minutes.
Director, executive producer, story, editor: Morrissey.
Producer: Andy Warhol.

Associate producer: Jed Johnson.
Camera operator: Warhol, Jed Johnson.
Sound: Jed Johnson.
Cast: Jackie Curtis (Jackie), Candy Darling (Candy), Holly Woodlawn (Holly), Marty Kove (Marty), Maurice Braddell (Candy's father), Duncan MacKenzie (Duncan, Candy's brother), Jonathan Kramer (journalist), Johnny Kemper (Johnny Minute), Michael Sklar (Max Morris), Sean O'Meara (Mrs. Fitzpatrick), Jane Forth (Jane, Mrs. Fitzpatrick's niece), George Abagnolo (photographer), Dusty Springs (Jackie's houseboy), Paul Kilb (Jackie's first boyfriend), Geri Miller, Brigid Polk (PIG women).

Heat, 103 minutes.
Director, story, screenplay, photography, camera operator: Morrissey.
Based on an idea by John Hallowell.
Producer: Andy Warhol.
Editors: Lara Jokel, Jed Johnson, Morrissey.
Music: John Cale.
Cast: Joe Dallesandro (Joe), Sylvia Miles (Sally), Andrea Feldman (Jessie), Pat Ast (motel owner), Ray Vestal (producer), Lester Persky (Sidney), Eric Emerson (Eric), Gary Koznocha (Gary), Harold Childe (Harold), Pat Parlemon, Bonnie Walder, John Hallowell.

1972
L'Amour, 90 minutes.
Director, story: Morrissey.
Producer: Warhol.
Assistant producer: Fred Hughes.
Production assistant, photography: J. J. Flori.
Camera operator: Warhol, Jed Johnson.
Editor: Lana Jokel, Jed Johnson.
Music: Ben Weisman. Lyrics: Michael Sklar. Song recorded by Cass Elliott.
Cast: Michael Sklar (Michael), Donna Jordan (Donna), Jane Forth (Jane), Max Delys (Max), Patti d'Arbanville (Patti), Karl Lagerfeld (Karl), Coral Labrie (Coral), Peter Greenlaw (Peter), Corey Tippin (Corey).

1973
Flesh for Frankenstein (Carne per Frankenstein, Italy/France), 95 minutes.
Director, story, screenplay: Morrissey.
Producers: Jean Pierre Rassam, Andrew Braunsberg, Carlo Ponti.
Production manager: Mara Blasetti.
Photography: Luigi Kuveiller.
Camera operator: Baldo Terzano.
Editors: Franca Silvi, Jed Johnson.
Production designer: Enrico Job.
Music composition and direction: Claudio Gizzi.
Spacevision 3-D, technical consultant: Robert V. Bernier.
Cast: Joe Dallesandro (Nicholas), Monique Van Vooren (Katrin Frankenstein), Udo

Kier (Baron Frankenstein), Arno Juerging (Otto), Carla Mancini (daughter), Marco Liofredi (son), Dalila Di Lazzaro (female monster), Srdjan Zelenovic (male monster), Nicoletta Elmi, Fiorella Masselli, Liu Bosisio (maid), Rosita Torosh, Cristina Gaioni, Imelde Marani.

Blood for Dracula (Dracula vuole vivere: cerca sangue di vergine!, Italy/France), 103 minutes.
Director, story, screenplay: Morrissey.
Producers: Jean Pierre Rassam, Andrew Braunsberg, Carlo Ponti.
Production manager: Mara Blasetti.
Photography: Luigi Kuveiller.
Camera operator: Baldo Terzano.
Editors: Jed Johnson, Franca Silvi.
Production designer: Enrico Job.
Music composition and direction: Claudio Gizzi.
Cast: Joe Dallesandro (Mario), Udo Kier (Dracula), Maxime McKendry (Marquise Di Fiori), Vittorio De Sica (Marquis Di Fiori), Arno Juerging (Anton), Milena Vukotic (Esmeralda), Dominique Darrell (Saphiria), Stefanie Carsini (Rubinia), Silvia Dionisio (Perla), Roman Polanski (villager).

1977
Hound of the Baskervilles, The, 85 minutes.
Director: Morrissey.
Executive producers: Michael White, Andrew Braunsberg.
Producer: John Goldstone.
Screenplay: Peter Cook, Dudley Moore, and Morrissey, based on the novel by Arthur Conan Doyle.
Photography: Dick Bush, John Wilcox.
Editors: Richard Marden, Glenn Hyde.
Production designer: Roy Smith.
Music: Dudley Moore.
Cast: Peter Cook (Sherlock Holmes), Dudley Moore (Dr. Watson, Mrs. Ada Holmes, Mr. Spiggot), Denholm Elliott (Stapleton), Joan Greenwood (Beryl Stapleton), Terry-Thomas (Dr. Mortimer), Max Wall (Arthur Barrymore), Irene Handl (Mrs. Barrymore), Kenneth Williams (Sir Henry Baskerville), Hugh Griffith (Frankland), Dana Gillespie (Mary Frankland), Roy Kinnear (Ethel Seldon), Prunella Scales (Glynis), Penelope Keith (massage receptionist), Spike Milligan (policeman), Lucy Griffiths (Iris), Jessie Matthews (Mrs. Tindale), Rita Webb, Mohammed Shamsi, and Patsy Smart (masseuses), Geoffrey Moon (Perkins), Josephine Tewson, Vivien Neve, and Jacquie Stevens (nuns), Anna Wing (Daphne), Henry Woolf (shopkeeper), Molly Maureen (Mrs. Oviatt), Helena McCarthy (Enid), Ava Cadell (Marsha), Sidney Johnson and Pearl Hackney (rail passengers).

1981
Madame Wang's, 95 minutes.
Director, story, screenplay, camera operator: Morrissey.
Producer: Jack Simmons.

Associate producer: Dan Woodruff.
Photography: Juan Drago, Jim Tynes.
Editor: George Wagner, Michael Nallin.
Cast: Patrick Schoene (Lutz), Christina Indri, William Edgar, Susan Blond, Jimmy Madaus, Virginia Bruce (Madame Wang). Performers: Leroy and the Lifters, Phranque, Mentors, Butch, Boneheads.

1982
Forty-Deuce, 90 minutes.
Director, screenplay: Morrissey.
Producer: Jean-Jacques Fourgeaud.
Production manager: Elliott Hoffman.
Production associate: Pierre Cottrell.
Photography: Steven Fierberg.
Camera crew: François Reichenbach, Stephan Zapasnik, Bruno Lapostolle.
Editor: Ken Eluto.
Music: Manu Dibango.
Cast: Kevin Bacon (Ricky), Mark Keyloun (Blow), Orson Bean (Mr. Roper), Harris Laskowy (Augie), Tommy Citera (Crank), Carol Jean Lewis (coke dealer), Esai Morales (Mitchell), Bo Rucker (coke dealer). Susan Blond, John Noonan, Yukio Yamamoto, Meade Roberts (man in street), Dave Kris, Rudy de Bellis (men in toilet).

1984
Mixed Blood (Cocaine, France), 99 minutes.
Director: Morrissey.
Executive producer: Alaine Sarde.
Producer: Antoine Gannage, Steven Fierberg.
Screenplay: Morrissey. Additional dialogue: Alan Bowne.
Associate producer: Mark Slater.
Photography: Stefan Zapasnik.
Editor: Scott Vickery.
Music: "Sugar Coated" Andy Hernandez.
Songs: "Amanecer" by Jose Gallardo, performed by Mongo Santamaria. "Che Che Cole" by Willie Colon, "Noche De Farra" by Armando M. Dwolff, "Songoro Consongo" by E. Grenet and N. Guillen, performed by Hector Lavoe. "El Africano" by Calixto Ochoa, performed by Wilfrido Vargas. "Tico Tico" by Z. Abreu and A. Oliveira, performed by Marilla Pera.
Cast: Maceteros: Marilla Pera (Rita La Punta), Richard Ulacia (Thiago), Geraldine Smith (Toni), Rodney Harvey (José), Alvaro Rodriguez (Herman), William Rodriguez (Carlos), Eduardo Gonzalez (Jajo), Steven Garcia (Pedro), Edwina Ebron (hooker), Andres Castillo (Michael Medina), Peter Cruz (Steven Medina), Richard Garcia (Andrew Pena), Emanuelle La Salle (Gary Peterson), John Leguizamo (Andres Rodriguez), Julian Lun Pen (Eric Rodriguez), Joselyn Marcano (Oscar Rodriguez Jr.), Ralph Martinez (Thomas Rosario), Daniel Martinez (Robert Vega); Master Dancers: Angel David (Juan the Bullet), Pedro Sanchez (Comanche), Fabio Urena (Stingray), Bobby Martinez (junkie guard), Christian DeFiris, Ricardo Caimares, Anthony Freire, and Roberto Santano (assassins), William Martinez (pool player),

John Curet (dealer at table), Isaac Manga (Leroy Andino), Roland Ptero (Paul Arguinzoni), Arturo Rodriguez (Sterling Campbell), Carlos Rodriguez (Santos Collado), John Rodriguez (Edgar Gonzalez), Abdel Saez (Ramon Gonzalez), Arthur W. H. Smith (Carlos Jimenez); outsiders: Linda Kerridge (Carol), Ulrich Berr (The German), Marcelino Rivera (Hector), Yukio Yamamoto (Captain Kenzo), Carol Jean Lewis (woman cop), Robert Badillo (Ted the cop), Jerry Conklin (Ted's partner), Susan Blond (caterer), Pelati Pons (mortician), Art Boulogne (complaining junkie), Toby Record (boy dealer in car), Patrick Indri (Pee Wee), Holger Pohlman (bartender), Xavier Santana (Toni's street lover), Susy Ramirez and Adolfo Posada (companions), Albert Lee Flecha (Teatro director), Ronnie Berman, Christel-Marie Guerra, Sandra Lewis, Richie Stewart, and Mario Fernandez (Teatro actors), Jessy Etheredge (cop at meeting), Steve Baker (detective), Jeremiah Hawkins (grammarian cop), Margarita Morales (screaming woman), Bobby (junkie on line).

1985

Beethoven's Nephew (Germany/France), 103 minutes.
Director: Morrissey.
Producer: Marita Coustet.
Screenplay: Morrissey, Mathieu Carrière, from the novel by Luigi Magnani, and the Beethoven *Conversation Books*.
Art Director: Mario Garbuglia.
Photography: Hanus Polak.
Editors: Albert Jurgenson, Michele Lauliac.
Musical advisors: Elena Rostropovitch, Pieter Daniel.
The Music: Sonata for Violin and Piano no. 5 (The Springtime Sonata), op. 24, performed by Wilhelm Kempf, piano; Yehudi Menuhin, violin. Sonata for Piano no. 13, op. 27, performed by Elena Rostropovitch. Quartet no. 13, op. 130, performed by Pieter Daniel, first violin; Yumiko Noda, second violin; Jaap Zeidl, viola; Wolfram Geiss, violoncello. Ninth Symphony, third and fourth movements, op. 125, performed by the Vienna Philharmonic with the State Opera Chorus conducted by Karl Boehm.
Cast: Wolfgang Reichmann (Ludwig van Beethoven), Dietmar Prinz (Karl), Jane Birkin (Johanna van Beethoven), Nathalie Baye (Leonore), Mathieu Carrière (Archduke Rodolphe), Ulrich Berr (Anton Schindler), Erna Korhel (Marie), Pieter Daniel (Karl Holz), Elena Rostropovitch (Countess Erdody), Walter Schupfer (Michael), Hellmuth Hron (Schoolmaster), David Cameron (The judge), Hubert Kramar (Johann van Beethoven).

1988

Spike of Bensonhurst, 101 minutes.
Director, story: Morrissey.
Executive producer: Sam Grogg.
Producer: David Weisman, Nelson Lyon.
Screenplay: Morrissey, Alan Bowne.
Photography: Steven Fierberg.
Editor: Stan Salfas.
Production designer: Stephen McCabe.

Songs: Pupo ("Malattia d'Amore," "Tu Amico Mio," "Ciao," "La Mia Anima," "E' Facile," "Notte Chiara," "Cieli Azzutti"); Massimo Ranieri ("Vent Anni"); Gianni Morandi ("La Mia Nemica"); Ricci e Poveri ("Sara Perche Ta Amo," "M'Innamoro Di Te," "Se M'Innamoro," "Made in Italy"); Fernandito Villalona ("Soy Dominicana").

Cast: Sasha Mitchell (Spike Fumo), Ernest Borgnine (Baldo Cacetti), Anne DeSalvo (Sylvia Cacetti), Sylvia Miles (congresswoman), Geraldine Smith (Helen Fumo), Antonia Rey (Bandana's mother), Rick Aviles (Bandana), Maria Pitillo (Angel), Karen Shallo (Blondie), Chris Anthony Young (Carmine), Mario Todisco (Tortorella), Rodney Harvey (Frankie), Taliso Soto (India), Frank Adonis (Vinaca), Frankie Gio (Pete Fumo), Robert Compono (Chicago Boxer), Tony Goodstone (Mafia boss), Justin Lazard (Justin), Carol Jean Lewis, Tommy Citera (junkies), Paul Dillon, Mark Tenore (cops), Angel David (teen dealer), Ron Maccone (D.A.'s man), Mary Lou Rosato (Italian mother), Patrick Indri (Italian son), Tommy Clark (prison guard), Ray Iannicelli (photographer), John Capodice (Mafia eater), Arlene Miyazaki (cashier), Ida Bernadini (grandmother), Michael Acciarito (Spike's brother), Steve Baker (dealer), Sal Viviano (singer), Anthony Bishop (video boss), Robert Mantana (bouncer), Ralph Monaco (Mafia man), Tony La Fortezza (Mafia stooge), Gene Amoroso (booth guard), Larry Ramos (referee), Michael Turney (Bar mitzvah boy), Jason Cerbone, Matthew Cerbone, Nicky Feliciano, Nick Gionta, Fabio Urena, Christian Saffran, Michael Dallesandro (gang members), Steven Shubert, Victora Preminger (soap stars), Rutger Gat (Spike Jr.).

Additional Films Cited

Airport, dir. George Seaton (1969)
Amadeus, dir. Milos Forman (1984)
Bad, dir. Jed Johnson (1976)
Bad Boys, dir. Rick Rosenthal (1983)
Bicycle Thief, The, (Ladri di biciclette), dir. Vittorio De Sica (Italy, 1948)
Bitter Rice (Riso amaro), dir. Giuseppe De Santis (Italy, 1948)
Blow Job, dir. Andy Warhol (1964)
Blue Angel, The, (Der blaue Angel), dir. Joseph von Sternberg (Germany, 1930)
Blue Movie, dir. Andy Warhol (1968)
Carnal Knowledge, dir. Mike Nichols (1971)
Christiane F. (Christiane F. wir Kinder vom Bahnhof Zoo), dir. Ulrich Edel (West
    Germany, 1981)
Cool World, The, dir. Shirley Clarke (1963)
Dial M For Murder, dir. Alfred Hitchcock (1954)
Diner, dir. Barry Levinson (1982)
Dionysus '69, dir. Brian De Palma, Robert Fiore, and Bruce Rubin (1970)
Easy Rider, dir. Dennis Hopper (1969)
Empire, dir. Andy Warhol (1964)
Exorcist, The, dir. William Friedkin (1973)
Fallen Idol, The, dir. Carol Reed (U.K., 1948)
Five Easy Pieces, dir. Bob Rafelson (1970)
Friday the 13th, dir. Sean Cunningham (1980)

Girls About Town, dir. George Cukor (1931)
Gone With the Wind, dir. Victor Fleming (1939)
Harlot, dir. Andy Warhol (1964)
Horse, dir. Andy Warhol (1965)
House of Wax, dir. Andre de Toth (1953)
I Am Curious (Yellow), dir. Vilgot Sjoman (Sweden, 1969)
La dolce vita (The Sweet Life), dir. Federico Fellini (Italy/France, 1960)
Last Tango in Paris, dir. Bernardo Bertolucci (Italy/France, 1972)
Macbeth, dir. Roman Polanski (U.K., 1971)
Man Between, The, dir. Carol Reed (U.K., 1953)
M*A*S*H, dir. Robert Altman (1969)
Midnight Cowboy, dir. John Schlesinger (1969)
Miracle in Milan (Miracolo a Milano), dir. Vittorio De Sica (Italy, 1950)
More Milk Yvette (aka Lana Turner), dir. Andy Warhol (1965)
My Hustler, dir. Andy Warhol (1965)
Nosferatu (Nosferatu – eine Symphonie des Grauens), dir. F. W. Murnau (Germany, 1923)
Odd Man Out, dir. Carol Reed (U.K., 1947)
Our Man in Havana, dir. Carol Reed (U.K., 1960)
Outcast of the Islands, dir. Carol Reed (U.K., 1951)
Outlaw, The, dir. Howard Hughes (1943)
Pixote (Pixote a lei do mais fraco) dir. Hector Babenco (Brazil, 1981)
Portrait of Jason, dir. Shirley Clarke (1967)
Pull My Daisy, dir. Robert Frank, Alfred Leslie (1960)
Rebel Without a Cause, dir. Nicholas Ray (1955)
Rocky, dir. John Avildsen (1976)
Romeo and Juliet, dir. Franco Zeffirelli (U.K., 1968)
Rules of the Game, The (La règle du jeu), dir. Jean Renoir (France, 1939)
Running Man, The, dir. Carol Reed (U.K., 1963)
Saturday Night Fever, dir. John Badham (1977)
Shadows, dir. John Cassavetes (1959)
Sleep, dir. Andy Warhol (1964)
Some Like it Hot, dir. Billy Wilder (1959)
Space, dir. Andy Warhol (1965)
Star Wars, dir. George Lucas (1977)
Straw Dogs, dir. Sam Peckinpah (U.K., 1971)
Sunset Boulevard, dir. Billy Wilder (1950)
Things to Come, dir. William Cameron Menzies (U.K., 1936)
Third Man, The, dir. Carol Reed (U.K., 1949)
Tootsie, dir. Sydney Pollack (1982)
Torch Song Trilogy, dir. Paul Bogart (1988)
Trip, The, dir. Roger Corman (1967)
2001: A Space Odyssey, dir. Stanley Kubrick (U.K., 1968)
Umberto D, dir. Vittorio De Sica (Italy, 1952)
Wavelength, dir. Michael Snow (Canada, 1967)
Wind from the East (Vent d'est), dir. Jean-Luc Godard (Italy/France/West Germany, 1970)

Bibliography

Allan, Blaine. "The Beat, The Hip, and The Square." In *Film Reader 5*, eds. Jae Alexander et al. Evanston, Illinois: Northwestern University Press, 1982, pp. 257–68.

Bailey, David. *Andy Warhol: Transcript of the ATV Documentary.* London: Bailey Litchfield/Matthews Miller Dunbar Ltd., 1972.

Beale, Lewis. "Paul Morrissey on *Trash.*" *Daily Planet,* 2, no. 2 (January 19–27, 1971), 3–5.

Bell-Metereau, Rebecca. *Hollywood Androgyny.* New York: Columbia University Press, 1985.

Bertolucci, Bernardo. *Last Tango in Paris.* New York: Dell, 1973.

Biro, Yvette. *Profane Mythology: The Savage Mind of the Cinema,* trans. Imre Goldstein. Bloomington: Indiana University Press, 1982.

Bockris, Victor, and Gerard Malanga. *Up-tight: The Velvet Underground Story.* London: Omnibus, 1983.

Bourdon, David. *Warhol.* New York: Abrams, 1989.

Byron, Stuart. "Reactionaries in Radical Drag." *Village Voice* (March 16, 1972), 69.

Cipnik, Dennis J. "Andy Warhol: Iconographer." *Sight and Sound* (Summer 1972), 158–61.

Colacello, Bob. *Holy Terror: Andy Warhol Close Up.* New York: Harper Collins, 1990.

Coplans, John, ed. *Andy Warhol.* New York: New York Graphic Society, 1978.

Curtis, David. *Experimental Cinema.* New York: Dell, 1971.

Dawes, Melton S. "Morrissey – From *Flesh* and *Trash* to *Blood for Dracula,*" *New York Times* (July 15, 1973).

Dienstfrey, Harris. "The New American Cinema," *Commentary,* 6, no. 33 (June 1962), 495–502.

Ehrenstein, David. "The Filmmaker as Homosexual Hipster: Andy Warhol Contextualized." *Arts Magazine* (Summer 1989), 61–4.

Evans, Walter. "Monster Movies: A Sexual Theory." In *Movies and Artifacts: Cul-*

tural Criticism of Popular Films, eds. Michael Marsden, John Nachbar, Sam Grogg Jr. Chicago: Nelson-Hall, 1982, pp. 129–36.

Fieschi, J. "Paul Morrissey." *Cinematographe,* no. 83 (November 1982), 36–8.

"Film-Makers' Co-operative Catalogue," *Film Culture* (Summer 1965), insert pp. 1–70.

Finkelstein, Nat. *Andy Warhol: The Factory Years, 1964–1967.* New York: St. Martin's, 1989.

Flamm, Matthew. "*Trash*-ing Beethoven," *New York Post* (June 9, 1988), 35.

Flatley, Guy. "He Enjoys Being a Girl." *New York Times* (November 15, 1970).

Ford, Greg. "*Trash.*" *Cinema (L.A.),* 7, no. 2 (Spring 1972), 54–6.

"You name it, I'll eat it." *Cinema (L.A.),* no. 33 (Spring 1973), 30–7.

Gardner, Paul. "Morrissey Gives the Director's View." *New York Times,* November 14, 1972.

Garrels, Gary, ed. *The Work of Andy Warhol.* Dia Art Foundation Discussions in Contemporary Culture, no. 3. Seattle: Bay Press, 1989.

Gelmis, Joseph. *The Film Director as Superstar.* New York: Doubleday, 1970.

Gibbons, William. "Conscience of a Post-Warhol Conservative." *Movieline* (November 4, 1988), 37, 61.

Glicksman, Marlaine. "Mellow Miles." *Film Comment* (August 1988), 55–9.

Godard, Jean-Luc. *Weekend/Wind from the East.* New York: Simon and Schuster, 1972.

Hanhardt, John G. *The Films of Andy Warhol: An Introduction.* New York: Whitney Museum, 1988.

Harmsworth, Madeleine. "*Flesh,*" *Sunday Mirror* (April 4, 1971).

Hoberman, J. "Mambo Dearest." *Village Voice* (November 22, 1988), 59, 68.

Howton, F. William. "Filming Andy Warhol's *Trash.*" *Filmmakers Newsletter,* 5, no. 8 (June 1972), 24–8.

Indiana, Gary. "Aces the Deuce: An Interview with Paul Morrissey." *East Village Eye* (March 1983), 8.

James, David E. "The Producer as Author," *Wide Angle,* 7, no. 3 (November 1985), 24–33.

Allegories of Cinema: American Film in the Sixties. Princeton, N.J.: Princeton University Press, 1989.

Johnson, William. "*Beethoven's Nephew.*" *Film Quarterly* (Fall 1988), 37–9.

Joseph, Peter. *Good Times: An Oral History of America in the Nineteen Sixties.* New York: Charterhouse, 1973.

Kael, Pauline. *Deeper Into Movies.* New York: Little Brown, 1973.

5001 Nights at the Movies. New York: Holt, Rinehart and Winston, 1982.

Kelman, Ken. "Anticipations of the Light." *The Nation* (May 11, 1964), 409–14.

Kinder, Marsha, and Beverle Houston. *Close-Up: A Critical Perspective on Film.* New York: Harcourt Brace Jovanovich, 1972.

"Woman and Manchild in the Land of Broken Promise: Ken Russell's *Savage Messiah* and Paul Morrissey's *Heat,*" in *Women and Film,* 1, nos. 3–4 (1973), 31–7.

Knode, Helen. "Sweet Bird of Youth." *L.A. Weekly* (July 17, 1988), 41.

"That 'L' Word." *L.A. Weekly* (November 18–24, 1988), 45–6.

Kobal, John. "Paul Morrissey: Life After Warhol." *Films and Filming* (June 1986), 16–17.

Koch, Stephen. *Stargazer: Andy Warhol's World and His Films.* New York: Praeger, 1973.

Kramer, Margia. *Andy Warhol et al.: The FBI File on Andy Warhol.* New York: UnSub Press, 1988.

Kuhn, Annette. *The Power of the Image: Essays on Representation and Sexuality.* London: Routledge & Kegan Paul, 1985.

Lambert, Gavin. *On Cukor.* New York: Capricorn, 1972.

Larson, Roger. "An Innocence, An Originality, a Clear Eye: A Retrospective Look at the Films of D.W. Griffith and Andy Warhol." *The Film Journal,* 1, nos. 3–4 (Fall–Winter 1972), 80–8.

Lavalle, Patrick. "New York 42 Rue," *Cinéma* (Paris), (December 1982), 84–5.

Lyons, Donald. "One-Way Ticket to Morrisseyville." *Details* (November 1988), 172–3.

Marcorelles, Louis. *Living Cinema: New Directions in Contemporary Film-Making.* London: George Allen and Unwin, 1973.

McCormack, Ed. "Only PIGS Could Follow Trash." *Inter/VIEW,* 2, no. 2 (1972), 23–5.

McLuhan, Marshall, and Quentin Fiore. *The Medium is the Massage: An Inventory of Effects.* New York: Bantam, 1967.

McShine, Kynaston, ed. *Andy Warhol: A Retrospective.* New York: Museum of Modern Art, 1989.

Mekas, Jonas. "Notes on the New American Cinema." *Film Culture,* 24 (Spring 1962), 6–16.

   "Movie Journal." *Village Voice* (September 29, 1966), 27.

   Movie Journal: The Rise of a New American Cinema, 1959–1971. New York: Collier, 1972.

   "Notes After Reseeing the Movies of Andy Warhol." In *Andy Warhol,* ed. John Coplans. New York: New York Graphic Society, 1978, pp. 139–57.

Mellen, Joan. *Women and their Sexuality in the New Film.* New York: Horizon, 1973.

Michener, Charles. "Put-on Artist." *Newsweek* (September 23, 1974), 89–91.

Milne, Tom, ed. *The Time Out Film Guide.* London: Penguin, 1989.

Montesano, Anthony P. "Spiked Punch." *American Film* (September 1988), 70.

Morrissey, Paul, et al., eds. *Andy Warhol's Index Book.* New York: Random House, 1967.

Morrissey, Paul. *Dialogue on Film.* American Film Institute. 4, no. 2 (November 1974), 20–32.

Morrissey, Paul, with Brigid Berlin. "Factory Days." In *Interview,* February, 1989, 57–61.

O'Pray, Michael, ed. *Andy Warhol Film Factory.* London: British Film Institute, 1989.

Pally, Marcia. "The New York Newsday Interview with Paul Morrissey." *Newsday* (February 2, 1989).

Pomeroy, Ralph. "An Interview with Andy Warhol." *Afterimage,* no. 2 (Autumn 1970), 34–41.

Ratcliff, Carter. *Andy Warhol*. New York: Abbeville, 1983.
Rayns, Tony. "Andy Warhol Films Inc.: Communication in Action." *Cinema* (U.K.),
    6–7 (August 1970), 42–7.
    "Bike Boy." Monthly Film Bulletin (December 1970), 243–4.
    "Chelsea Girls." Monthly Film Bulletin (July 1972), 134–5.
    "Trash." Monthly Film Bulletin (February 1973), 38.
    "Women in Revolt." Monthly Film Bulletin (August 1973), 179.
Renoir, Jean. *The Rules of the Game*. London: Lorrimer, 1970.
Robinson, David. "When is a Dirty Film . . . ?" *Sight and Sound* (Winter 1971–2),
    28–30.
Rosenbaum, Jonathan. *Film: The Front Line*. Denver: Arden, 1983.
Samuels, Charles Thomas. *Encountering Directors*. New York: Putnam, 1972.
Sarris, Andrew. "Film: *The Chelsea Girls*," *Village Voice* (December 15, 1966), 33.
Scott, Jay. "The Wacky, Irreverent Orbit of Paul Morrissey." (Toronto) *Globe and
    Mail* (November 11, 1988).
Simon, John. *Reverse Angle: A Decade of American Films*. New York: Potter, 1982.
Sitney, P. Adams. *Visionary Film: The American Avant-Garde*. New York: New
    York University Press, 1978.
Smith, Patrick S. *Andy Warhol's Art and Films*. Ann Arbor, Michigan: UMI Research
    Press, 1986.
    Warhol: Conversations About the Artist. Ann Arbor, Michigan: UMI Research
    Press, 1988.
Stein, Jean. *Edie: An American Biography*. New York: Dell, 1982.
Tarratt, Margaret. *"Flesh."* Films and Filming (April 1970), 42–3.
    "Heat." Films and Filming (June 1973), 51–2.
Taylor, John Russell. "Paul Morrissey/*Trash*." *Sight and Sound* (Winter 1971–2),
    31–2.
    Directors and Directions: Cinema for the Seventies. London: Eyre Methuen,
    1975.
Thoms, Albie. *Polemics for a New Cinema*. Sydney: Wild and Woolley, 1978.
Thurman, Judith. "Paul Morrissey: A World of Images." *Architectural Digest* (May
    1990), 72–8.
Tyler, Parker. *Underground Film: A Critical History*. London: Penguin, 1971.
    Screening the Sexes: Homosexuality in the Movies. New York: Holt, Rinehart
    and Winston, 1973.
    *The Shadow of an Airplane Climbs the Empire State Building: A World Theory
    of Film*. New York: Anchor, 1973.
Ultra Violet. *Famous for 15 Minutes: My Years With Andy Warhol*. New York:
    Harcourt Brace Jovanovich, 1988.
Viva. *Superstar*. New York: Putnam, 1970.
    "Viva and God." *Village Voice* (May 5, 1987). Voice Art Supplement, 9.
Warhol, Andy. *a*. New York: Grove Press, 1968.
    Blue Movie. New York: Grove Press, 1970.
    From A to B and Back Again: The Philosophy of Andy Warhol. London: Michael
    Dempsey, 1975.
    The Andy Warhol Diaries. ed. Pat Hackett. New York: Warner, 1989.

and Pat Hackett. *Popism: The Warhol '60s*. New York: Harper and Row, 1980.

Weightman, John. "Flesh in the Afternoon." *Encounter* (June 1970), 30–2.

"All Flesh is Trash." *Encounter* (June 1971), 45–6.

"Minimal Relationships." *Encounter* (June 1973), 37–9.

Wilcock, John, ed. *The Autobiography and Sex Life of Andy Warhol*. New York: Other Scenes, 1971.

Winokur, Scott. "*Fusion* Interview: Paul Morrissey." *Fusion* no. 50 (February 19, 1971), 12–15.

Wolf, William. "From *Trash* to Riches." *Cue* (November 14, 1970), 13.

Youngblood, Gene. *Expanded Cinema*. New York: Dutton, 1970.

Zimmerman, Paul D. "*Andy Warhol's Frankenstein*." *Newsweek* (May 20, 1974), 105.

Index

Lightning Source UK Ltd.
Milton Keynes UK
UKOW04f0947150915

258659UK00001B/214/P